PASTORAL TRANSITIONS

FROM
ENDINGS
TO
NEW
BEGINNINGS

Wm. Bud Phillips

Published in collaboration with
the Centre for the Study of Church and Ministry

AN ALBAN INSTITUTE PUBLICATION

The Publications Program of The Alban Institute is assisted by a grant from Trinity Church, New York City.

Library of Congress Catalog Card Number 88-71755
ISBN #1-56699-029-7

CONTENTS

The study of the dynamic relationship between congregations and their pastoral leaders is one that has fascinated and challenged many of us who work within the church as consultants and teachers. There is simply no parallel to the symbiotic relationship, the ebb and flow of power, the elasticity of mutual responsibility and the resources of energy that have their roots beyond the institution itself. It is out of this fascination, and after twenty-five years of active participation in that dynamic, that I dare to write about what seems to be a mystery within the greater mystery: the fact that congregations of God's people and individuals of God's choosing find one another and work out the wonderful mutual commitment we call Ministry.

This book is not the exposition of a theology of Congregations nor of Ministry. It attempts merely to describe and analyze a single recurring phenomenon with the life experience of the congregation. What is offered here is the distillation of observations and insights gained from working in and with scores of congregations and their pastors when one pastor leaves and gives way to the coming of another.

I have experienced personal pastoral transitions in Edmonton, Alberta; Jerseyville and Toronto, Ontario; Saskatoon, Saskatchewan and Arlington, Massachusetts. In each of those places there were magnificent human beings who moved through the endings, interim period and beginnings with me in a spirit of grace and faithfulness.

William Bridges, who started to think about transitions because he heard and reflected upon the many personal changes in the lives of his students, has moved on to explore the shape of transitions in organizations and institutions. He provided a framework for my thinking about the transitions in congregations and it has led me to consider afresh the transitions in my own life and that of others. The understanding of the process of transitions is transferable from personal experience to congregational experience and back again. It is therefore appropriate to try to write for both clergy and for congregations simultaneously—appropriate but not always manageable.

The Bishop, Cabinet and leaders of the Pacific Northwest Conference of the United Methodist Church have provided many of the opportunities for the experiences needed to recognize and describe the elements of Endings, Interims and Beginnings. The many Transition Workshops, and individual Transition consultations they commissioned over the past five years have served to multiply my personal experiences.

I am grateful to my colleagues at the Vancouver School of Theology, who have allowed me to make personal transitions in my work in the administration and programs of the School. They have proven to be a most supportive community.

In observing, studying and experiencing the phenomena of pastoral change, I have come to appreciate anew the profound significance of the relationships of stability that support us in our times of transition. It is therefore with deep love and gratitude that I acknowledge my debt to my wife Kay, and our two children David and Deborah. They have frequently stood with me "in the interim" and always with grace, strength and love.

"Why are you leaving?"

Bob MacKenzie knew he would be asked that question many times in the three months between the announcement of his decision to accept a call to another church and the time he would actually leave. He had thought of a number of ways to answer it, but had come to realize that it would need to be answered differently for some people than for others.

What he was not prepared for was the silence. Some of his parishioners would never talk to him about it and some would never actually say good-bye. He did not fully anticipate how difficult it would be for them either to understand or accept his voluntary conclusion of an important relationship. Nor was he fully aware of his own mixed feelings.

There had been no obvious difference of opinion or conflict, no great dramatic change in the life and experience of his congregation, and no move to encourage him to relocate. In fact, in the minds of most of the church's members there was little reason for the decision and for the difficulty, confusion and prolonged period of disorganization that was sure to follow. Each time he heard the question, Bob would also come to recognize that behind it were various levels of anger, frustration, disappointment, anxiety, and guilt. Even those who tried to accept the change without judgment soon indicated their lack of clarity and understanding.

Sometimes the announcement of a pastoral change is made for obvious reasons. Those who hear it are very much aware of the reasons. Some people are relieved, some angry but sympathetic, some concerned for what it leaves unfinished and unsaid. In these cases there may well have been specific incidents, debates, confrontations,

or actions taken which could have been seen as the events which
precipitated the decision of a pastor to move.

In some ways the decision of a pastor to leave one church and
move to another is similar to that of a person in any other professional group. There are issues of professional development, family
needs and wants, changes of attitude, and shifts in the feeling of
"fit" between the pastor and his or her working conditions. While it
is often difficult to talk about (for reasons which will be discussed
later), pastors do seek increased earning potential, added prestige
and greater challenge. These often call for a move. The pastor's
motivation can be both complicated and shrouded by a conspiracy
of silence which may be one of the most difficult of career liabili-
ties.

One of the problems is the confusion as to who actually "calls" a
pastor to move. While there are different denominational systems
which are supposed to make the matter clearer and neater, in fact
these same systems can, themselves, be the cause of some of the
confusion. If it is stated that the call came from God and the decision to accept it came only after prayer and careful listening to the
Spirit, then who can debate it and who would attach invalid or inappropriate motives to the decision?

The symbiotic relationship between congregation and pastor
poses another problem. It is assumed that the church's goals, purposes and motives are mutually held. This assumption shatters
when the pastor decides to leave. The decision is often made unilat-
erally in response to outside influences or internal pressures. This
puts shared goals in jeopardy. The reactions that follow reflect the
mood of a group of people who feel deceived or at least have been
surprised into the awareness that the relationship was not what it
appeared to be.

In his study of the process of transitions through which we pass
whenever we experience a change of job, partnerships, location,
etc., William Bridges[1] notes that there seem to be three different
regions of feeling. The first region he calls "Endings" with its characteristic experiences of disenchantment, dis-identification, disorganization and disengagement. The second region he calls the
"Neutral Zone"—a time and space of measuring losses and establishing new directions. Finally, Bridges suggests we enter the region
of "New Beginnings," where we undertake the emotional work of
re-establishing enchantment, identity, organization and engagement
in our lives.

[1] William Bridges, *Transitions: Making Sense of Life's Changes* (Reading: Addison-
Wesley, 1980).

What follows is an example of the particular transition we call Pastoral Change. It is often a troubling experience because it involves many types of transition simultaneously. Not only does the pastor's job change but so does his or her location, and the sense of partnership with those who have shared a common vision and journey.

The book is written for four purposes:

To bring to word some of the feelings, confusions and complications which make this transition experience more difficult than it may need to be for both pastors and their congregations.

To establish some common categories and language to facilitate richer and deeper conversations between pastor and people about the shared experience which so profoundly affects about 20% of the churches in North America every year.

To encourage careful consideration of some of the causes and effects of pastoral change which may be one of the major factors for congregational passivity.

To explore ways of using the process of pastoral change to facilitate improved pastor/parish relationships.

It is also written with the hope that those who experience pastoral change—the pastors, their families, the leaders and members of a congregation—may come to consider it as an opportunity for the redevelopment of mission plans, the vitalization of congregational vision, and the clarification of intentions and purposes in everyone's ministry.

Beginning with Endings

No one ever really knows when endings begin and few, if any, can identify all of the reasons or implications related to the experience of "Endings."

We are engaged in observing, describing, and relating to a process which has many universal elements but which is usually felt to be a unique experience by both pastor and congregation. While it is possible to identify the characteristics of endings, as they are expressed in many pastoral changes, the feelings of those who go through the experience are quite personal, specific, and complex. They frequently defy easy classification.

The elements of *disenchantment, dis-identification* and *disorganization* have particular shape and sharpness when the ending under consideration is that of a pastoral relationship. The process of *disengagement* in the case of pastoral leave-taking has its own unique qualities if those separating from one another have shared common goals of ministry and mission and a common venture of faith. It is especially true that the phenomenon of oscillation--the human movement from intra-dependence to extra-dependence or vice versa--as initially suggested in another context has a peculiar and important function in the matter of pastoral change and in the process of endings.

It is to these situations that we must turn first.

CHAPTER 1

Disenchantment

The pastor had come to talk about his need for continuing education but it was clear that a deeper need was related to feelings
about himself and his work. "It just doesn't feel the same anymore.
I can't get as deeply involved or as excited about the church's program as I used to, and I think I'm feeling less sure that I *want* to."

It is difficult and even painful to try to talk about the feeling of
disenchantment with a particular situation of ministry. This is partly
because of a fear of where such conversations will lead and partly
because of a lack of clarity about the sources of our disenchantment. A search for the deepest meanings in this experience may be
the crucial step in avoiding mistakes at the time of pastoral change.

Sources of Disenchantment

Probably the most obvious focus for the source of disenchantment
is found in the pastor and within the congregation. Certainly those
sources require exploration but it will be helpful to look in other
directions as well. Some pastors do not feel they belong to their
denomination in the way they did a few years ago. The church,
besides its congregational manifestations has a "personality and
character" defined by national and international leaders and programs, by denominational papers and magazines and by public
statements, promotions and positions. Many pastors feel less clearly
affiliated then they did when they accepted ordination and began
their work.

Some pastors have been hurt by the people who give leadership
at the various levels of the church structure. Confidences have been
broken, leadership offers have been rejected, and carelessness in
administration by denominational staff has put pastors in embarrassing positions in relation to their congregations. There are stories of
the failure of the "system" to protect, defend or show support for

pastors who were trying to be faithful "between a rock and a hard place."

For a number of pastors the disenchantment began in theological school. The idealism, vision and energy engendered by a call to ministry seemed to fade amid the rigor of studies. The loss of support from the home congregation was a factor as was the growing discomfort created by the "over against" attitude that can exist between theological school and the church. Many seminary graduates feel that the church they serve is quite different from those described, assumed and prepared for in their theoretical and practical studies.

The fault cannot be located exclusively at the door of the theological school. Much of what passes for Christian nurture in the church is less than significant and fails to be faithful either to text or tradition. Such an education needs to be challenged, corrected and appraised—a process which can be disenchanting.

Some pastors had come to value and expect the same level of camaraderie and colleagueship which had been developed at theological school. It has never been the same since. In fact for some, the spirit of competition between churches and pastors even within the same denomination has led to a disenchantment of major proportions.

Disenchantment occurs for some in the first church appointment after theological school. Denominational procedures for orienting pastors to their ministry, while usually well meant, may neither consider the full implications of the transition from seminary to church nor the high level of supervision, support and orientation activities which are needed.

The personal profiles of clergy have changed in recent years. Now more than 50% of the graduates of theological schools in Canada have had a significant career before "hearing a call" and entering seminary. Nearly 50% of the candidates for ministry today are women. Both of these factors indicate issues and conditions which should profoundly influence the processes we use for orienting, introducing and supporting clergy.

The Local Church as Disenchanter

In almost every church there is some element which causes serious doubt as to whether the local congregation is a means of God's purpose and will in the world. Pastors are frustrated by the discovery that for many parishioners the church's ministry and mission start and stop with "their" need. The resistance to a wider vision of mission, to a deeper commitment to the poor or to the disadvantaged, and to the challenge presented by the third world and its needs is a disconcerting experience to many pastors. Others find they are frustrated because their parishioners show a lack of concern for the "unsaved," or for the destructive effects of pornography. Perhaps they seem to ignore other aspects of personal and social sin or they accept ethical decisions that are too easily assumed to be the result of "progress." Whether their stance is liberal or conservative, pastors have faced uneasy relationships with the general values of congregations they serve and at times the differences between them becomes intolerable.

There are other things too: the way that decisions are made, the relatively small number of people willing to give time and energy to leadership and ministry activity, the constant pressure on budgets and the consequent effect on salaries, support staff and working conditions all can and do lead to varying forms of disenchantment.

Of course it works both ways. Pastors who do not maintain or value denominational or congregational traditions, who do not keep confidences or who place parishioners in other embarrassing positions are cause for congregational disenchantment.

Those pastors who contribute to an unhealthy competitive spirit and who function as if they had no peers can contribute significantly to the disenchantment some congregational members feel toward them or the pastoral ministry in general.

Some congregations become disenchanted with a pastor who always seems to be leading them in ways they do not wish to go and/or confronting them with issues and concerns they believe to be neither essential to the work of the church nor a faithful response to the Gospel.

Unfortunately, many pastoral changes occur without an exit interview where feelings of mutual disenchantment can be acknowledged and discussed and where both the pastor and key lay leaders can learn from each other and reflect on their common experiences. A format for an exit interview will be outlined later.

Leadership Issues

Another matter which has emerged to cause some level of disenchantment relates to assumptions and expectations around leadership in the local congregation. To believe that all the people of God are called to ministry and all are encouraged to offer gifts of leadership is an ideal which may be easy to preach but difficult, if not impossible, to find in practice. For many people, the search for such an ideal congregation seems hopeless, and creating it is a much more difficult task for pastors than the theory about "enabling leadership" would suggest.

Most pastors do not experience the congregation as a gathering of people waiting to be enabled into a shared or mutual ministry. To be sure there are some, perhaps many people, in a congregation that are responsive to such an inspired concept, but there are many others, who are quite content to let the pastor and a few over-worked lay people supply the major vision, initiative and energy for ministry. One of the most disillusioning and disenchanting experiences for pastors is finally to come to realization that their major effort in ministry is more likely to be spent inspiring people to take their baptismal vow seriously, rather than in giving support to people who do.

Measuring the Pastor's Disenchantment

While disenchantment cannot be measured easily or precisely, it has at least two different and inter-related elements. The first has to do with the pastor's own sense of readiness for ministry which includes his or her gifts, skills, qualities and competencies for the task; these are the personal/professional factors. The second element can be described as the measure of confidence which the pastor feels about the church.

The pastors who would rank highest in the personal/professional scale would be those who sense that they have "the right stuff"— a deep and personal commitment to the church and the gospel, a number of years of training, experience, reflection and maturation, and enough support and encouragement from those who are "family." These pastors feel they have a realistic and adequate view of leadership and their role in it, a devotional or spiritual base from which to ride the disappointments and frustrations of professional ministry, and enough self-assurance with all of that to go on and serve through the various "sloughs of despond," "valleys of the shadow," and "dark nights of the soul" that are part of the journey of faithfulness.

Others feel less confident. They long for a return to the glorious days that gave them direction as a candidate for ministry. They feel uncertain about the way in which the Gospel is to be interpreted in this day when contexts seem so confusing. They wish there were more appropriate opportunities for colleague relationships and shared ministry, for support and nurture. They are not sure that what they know makes them adequate for the job. Continuing edu-

cation efforts may add even more frustration since they only serve
to emphasize the inadequacy of their training and preparedness, or
perhaps undermine the few certainties with which they work. They
lack confidence in their own skill and knowledge, and in their ability to apply them appropriately. On the scale of 1-10, measuring
personal/professional preparedness, such dispirited people would
rate below 5.

The second element of disenchantment is related to how much
a pastor feels a sense of confidence and faith in the church as a
vehicle of God's purpose and mission in the world. Some individuals have complete confidence in the efficacy of the church; their
experiences with and in the church have assured them that God is
not only able and willing but is indeed even now actually using the
church effectively and well. Such people trust the church as a vehicle of mission.

Others, while still trusting the church, have some misgivings.
They worry about the degree to which the church has capitulated to
forms of cultural captivity. They see attitudes within the church to
be so similar to those of the community at large that they search in
vain for the significant "Christian distinctives."

Still other pastors have a deep disillusionment about the church
that accepted, trained, appointed and supported them. For some
there seems so little difference in the church's role as to make its
separate existence from other community agencies irrelevant. For a
few the church is an embarrassment. They believe it not only fails
to reach its potential, but in fact takes positions and makes statements which are out of line with an intelligent and faithful interpretation of Scripture or tradition. For these people the church is no
longer a viable means of grace. By diagramming and comparing the
two factors—personal/professional readiness and confidence in the
church—some interesting and important distinctions emerge which
may help make the nature of disenchantment more clear.

A. The Confident Doubter

A pastor who trusts his or her own skills but has lost confidence in
the church may well be a candidate for a move out of the church
into some other career, or vocation. Some will find their way into
administration or teaching positions, believing that from that van-
tage point they may be able to strengthen the resources for congregations. If, however, they decide to stay in congregational ministry,
they will look for a move to a church that would rekindle hope and
confidence in the local congregation as a place in which God's purpose and mission may be fulfilled.

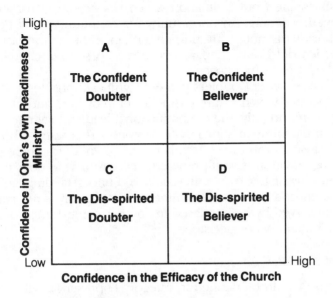

Confidence in the Efficacy of the Church

One pastor after serving a number of years in a particularly frustrating and depressing situation said, "I had to move to be healed." Such a condition puts great pressure on the lay leaders and the program leaders in the "receiving church." The issue here is nothing less than the possibility of losing a gifted and skilled pastor. The appropriate continuing education, reading and reflection which would assist in clarifying the role of the church in its culture, could support these pastors and also provide encouragement, energy and assurance for those offering leadership. Opportunities for colleagueship should be sought and encouraged.

B. *The Confident Believer*

Pastors who trust both their own competence and the church as a vehicle of God's work and witness are probably far more settled and less likely to move than those in any other category. Of course, as we shall see, there are other reasons for pastoral changes but they are not likely to be described by the term "disenchantment."

C. *The Dis-spirited Doubter*

Pastors who feel neither sure of the role and purpose of the church, nor of their ability to make a contribution as minister are in some ways most desperate. A move from one congregation to another is not particularly exciting or fulfilling except that it pro-

vides an escape from a situation which has become frustrating and
even overburdening. An opportunity for continuing education to
upgrade skills is not motivating either, since there is a basic feeling that it would only prepare one better to serve a church that
has little purpose or impact.

The Dis-spirited Doubters present significant problems for those
denominations which assure pastors of employment and placement.
But more importantly, the denominational leaders may need to be
careful in planning an appropriate response. The pastor who has
basically lost faith in the church is no gift to another congregation
unless the situation is well-prepared. The pastor who does not
believe in his or her own ability, skill and understanding, and
whose identity as a competent minister is not clear, is not particularly well-served by being placed in another congregation. It only
delays a much deeper decision.

D. The Dis-spirited Believer

Those who would be defined in category D present an altogether
different set of issues for themselves and the church. The Dis-spirited Believer is one who trusts the church as God's instrument, but
has low self esteem as a messenger, minister, teacher and enabler
of the faithful and needy.

The motivation to make a pastoral change for these clergy is
more clearly related to their self-dissatisfaction. Often they fear that
their inability will hinder the work of the church. Some honestly
believe their work is finished in a given place because they feel the
congregation has outgrown them or that their levels of skill and
knowledge are not up to the tasks presented by their congregation.
Although such people are less likely to leave the church as a vocational setting, they are more likely to move from one place to
another with little self satisfaction or enrichment.

Continuing education for Dis-spirited Believers should emphasize the development of knowledge and skills appropriate for the
work they are called to do. They do not need church-enhancing
experiences as much as they need minister-enhancing ones.

The Nature of Disenchantment

Disenchantment takes place at many levels—often simultaneously—
and unless some care is taken at the time of pastoral change, little
is learned from the experience.

A number of congregations have found that an exit interview is helpful. After the announcement has been made and before the pastor actually leaves, a time is set aside for a non-judgmental conversation between the pastor and a few carefully selected representatives of a congregation. Of course the conversation may take many different forms, but some have found it helpful to have had any style of forum through which to examine the levels of disenchantment and a system of categories to explore the inter-relationships that have evolved. In this context, pastors often feel free to say specifically and directly what were the major reasons behind a decision to move. Key lay leaders are also able to identify and articulate those elements of pastoral and congregational life which they believe require critical reflection by the pastor.

It is often helpful to have a third party involved in assisting the management of the conversational flow and assuring that "listening" and "hearing" becomes a mutually supportive experience. A person who is both objective and interested, and who is mutually trusted, could be most valuable.

A number of aspects of the nature of disenchantment may be fruitfully discussed at an exit interview. First it is useful to examine the *location* at which the feelings of disenchantment are experienced. They may be located at the personal, congregational or systemic level. Is it the pastor's disenchantment or those of individuals within the congregation? Are people feeling a general malaise within the congregation at large or is the disenchantment with the denominational system, structures and attitudes?

Next, it is valuable to focus on the *source* or cause of disenchantment. It may be rooted in the life of the congregation, the nature and resources of the community, or in issues that are national and international in scope. Some pastors leave because of their feelings about the congregation but others see that the community no longer serves their needs or those of their family. Still others leave because they are troubled by the relation between the local church and the attitudes and positions taken by national church leaders on national issues.

A third aspect of the nature of disenchantment to be raised in an exit interview is the matter of *leadership expectations*—both those of the clergy and of the laity. What was expected of whom? How were these expectations articulated? Were they reasonable?

Yet another field of enquiry most suitable for an exit interview is that of the *assumptions and definitions of "mission"* as held by both clergy and lay leaders. Disenchantments can arise as a result of differing views of the meaning of the mission and purpose of the church. An exit interview can be a "teachable moment" and provide an uncluttered time for both clergy and laity to hear one another.

Dealing with Disenchantment

If handled well, a careful discussion and disclosure of the experience of disenchantment in a pastoral relationship can yield insight, growth and development both for the congregation and the pastor. It never seems appropriate for responsible, committed, dedicated human beings to separate from one another without caring for the institution they have mutually labored to develop and protect. Perhaps the highest compliment either pastor or congregation can pay to one another is that expressed by taking each other's level of disenchantment seriously. These discussions are also freeing. They allow pastors to move to new places of work and service feeling that what was accomplished has been understood and accepted and what was not has been identified, acknowledged and owned as a continuing responsibility. Saying goodbye to a pastor can be a more satisfying and growth producing experience if both parties have taken the opportunity to reflect deeply and significantly upon the shared concerns, deep visions and hopes, and mutual responsibilities that make up a pastor/parish relationship.

CHAPTER 2

Dis-Identification

Our pastor spends a great deal of time in the city. It seems he's always over there at the denominational office working on one committee or another.

While some may consider it a matter of prestige that their pastor is consulted on major issues facing the wider church, most people who use words like these are expressing certain levels of discontent and dissatisfaction. They are concerned that their pastor seems distracted from what they believe to be his or her principal task—the work in the local church. They are pointing to a condition that may be called "Dis-identification"—the situation where the pastor draws a part of his or her identity from activities and services which are not clearly and directly related to the local church or where he or she is not necessarily totally committed to the tasks and functions in that one place.

Some pastors accused of being detached are puzzled because they believe their various commitments have an integrated unity which ultimately seems to center on the local church. Others accept the accusation as being a true statement of their feelings. They *do* find satisfaction and fascination with work outside the local church.

How an action is intended and how it is perceived is an important matter for discussion between the parties concerned.

Dis-identification becomes an issue when the activities of the pastor become diffuse and oblique. Sometimes pastors retain allegiance to their former church and their identification remains in their past. It gets expressed with phrases that look backwards, such as "It was better," "I was better. . ." "We did it better. . ." This may reflect reality, but the effect is to distance the pastor from his or her present congregation.

Often dis-identification comes as a result of a growing dream, that in the future there will be a fulfilling experience, when the pastor can work out more satisfactory answers to the identity questions:

"Who do I think I am?" "What do I think I can do and be?" and, "How do I think I should be used?"

The recognition of a different place of identification is often related to a growing sense of "call" in another direction. Some begin to feel called to graduate studies, some to work in areas of the church's ministry that are not based in the congregation. Still others feel that they have been prepared for service in denominational and interdenominational roles. They may wish to respond to a distant call to areas of mission endeavor on another continent. In these cases, the members of a congregation may find some satisfaction in the belief that their pastor is identified with other, appreciated ministries of the church. Nevertheless, some members will still feel frustrated and disappointed.

The signs may become obvious. They are often only thinly veiled and frequently become an irritant to those in the congregation who have maintained long-term membership.

One lay leader put it this way:

> We knew Karen was thinking of going to study for her doctorate, but we didn't know when. She wouldn't be specific. She got involved in discussions with universities and theological schools and spent a great deal of time reading and writing things that didn't seem related to what was going on here. We all loved her and encouraged her but it got disconcerting when she would be so obviously "somewhere else" when we needed her attention and commitment.

Other signs of dis-identification can become serious elements of discord and conflict. One pastor visited India as a member of his denomination's mission board delegation. He became so clearly identified with the needs and conditions of the people in a specific village in India that one parishioner observed: "It colored all his thinking, and dominated most of his attention. It made his preaching and teaching so predictable that most of us turned it off."

Not all dis-identification is found in the pastor. A major source of concern to pastors is the level of detachment they find in members of their congregations. The engagement and commitment of many parishioners to the church and God's purposes may only reflect a small fraction of that given to community activities, personal holidays, family matters and so on.

Dis-identification on the part of members of the congregation may take many forms: infrequent attendance, missed meetings, failure to follow through on commitments, indifference to the congregation's priorities, reduced giving and partial participation. Some of the early signs of congregational dis-identification are illustrated in these behavior patterns. Other people, however, simply start "church shopping," indicating that they do not feel as closely linked with their own church and pastoral leadership as they once did.

Categories of Dis-identification

A more precise definition of the types of dis-identification may help avoid superficiality in the discussions that take place between pastor and congregation at the time of pastoral change. Recognizing the varieties of feelings helps to provide appropriate and accurate language for evaluation, support and interpretation.

Subjective Dis-identification

Two weeks before he left to begin a ministry elsewhere, one pastor said he had never actually felt identified with his congregation. It is significant that he stated his feelings in the past tense:

> Somehow I was never "at home" here. It had something to do with the feeling of the place—it was like nothing I had ever known as a place of worship, and the ambiance was all wrong.

While vague and ill defined, the feelings were very strong and would not go away.

Some aspects of dis-identification are *subjective* in nature in that they are more related to emotion and feeling than any specific or objective reality. The language of "fit" is frequently used to describe the relationship between pastor and congregation. It has to do not only with the interplay between persons, but relates also to the harmony of theological position, political and social rapport, and the difference between expectations and response.

Subjective dis-identification can be a powerful force to weaken and even disable a pastoral relationship. After a very brief ministry, one lay leader quizzically commented, "Our pastor never made it into the hearts of our congregation. I don't know what it was. She wasn't radical, or abrasive, nor was she very different from the two pastors before her. Somehow she just didn't seem right for the job." After further consideration during a transition workshop held in the interim between pastors, it became obvious that many of the members were still emotionally identified with one or other of the pastor's predecessors, both of whom had been deeply loved and appreciated.

Dis-identification of the subjective type can be most disabling and enervating since it is often very difficult to indentify its source and focus.

Social Dis-identification

This relates to the cultural, relational and geographical conditions which may cause either a conflict of values or a disquieting sense of incongruity.

A pastor, raised in a major city, educated in another one, and serving as associate in an urban church, decided for family and health reasons to accept a call to a church in a prairie town. His early exclamations seem humorous in retrospect: "Nobody here ever reads the *Globe and Mail*!" The leaders of the congregation were equally chagrined that their new pastor, while he seemed intelligent enough, never seemed to know what was going on. The pastor has since learned that the *Globe and Mail* does not help him keep up with many of the important community concerns, but reading the local community newspaper does help and dropping in at the local store is an even better way of catching up with the news.

For some congregations the language, attitudes, natural responses and general demeanor of a pastor seem to place that person in a different social and cultural order from the people with whom he or she ministers. For some pastors the things that matter to their parishioners do not seem to be the things that matter to them.

Included in the list of elements that contribute to social dis-identification are discrepancies between pastor and people:

—family relationships and personal lifestyles

—friendship patterns and issues of loneliness

—the manner of communication and language

—worship forms and music appreciation

—ecumenical attitudes

—political and social values

—levels of social perception

Many congregations now take more seriously the possibility of social confusion in the early stages of a pastoral relationship. They plan, in the early months of a new ministry, to work intentionally to provide support and even oversight for the socializing of the new pastor and his or her family. Without a successful process of socialization the continuing dis-identification becomes detrimental to an effective ministry.

Professional Dis-identification

This is a category that includes the many disquieting feelings of distance and/or discrepancy which result from the different expectations of roles and functions within the church.

The pastor has certain ways of acting as leader, interpreter, teacher and administrator, and these can be at odds with the role identity that has been established over many years of pastor/parish relationships in a congregation. Pastors also come to identify the roles and functions of ministry with certain levels of authority and power. These can vary from congregation to congregation. Frequently the sources of estrangement can be found in perceptions of misunderstood authority and misused power.

Professional identity has been explored by many students of pastoral ministry. The stress created by discrepancies of understanding about the roles of leadership, can be a major cause for pastoral discomfort if not pastoral change. On the personal level some pastors report a deep feeling of anomie rooted in the confusion of roles created by a new awareness of the ministry of the whole people of God. This welcome concept has emerged without a parallel articulation of the special and significant nature of the ministry of those who are ordained by congregation and/or episcopacy for a particular part of the church's ministry.

Recent graduates of theological schools experience the problem in reverse. They have been educated, socialized and encouraged to understand that the ministry of the church is a shared, mutual and cooperative endeavor. Frequently when they arrive at their first appointment they discover that for the most part, members of the congregation understand the ministry to be the job of the clergy, so they tend to disassociate themselves with a concept of ministry that places a high level of expectation and responsibility on them.

Theological Dis-identification

Some of the dis-identification noted in pastor/parish relationships clearly has its roots in theological differences.

After an effective and well-received ministry of six years, one young pastor announced he was leaving to take a year's "study and reflection time." In private conversation he described some of the anxiety and concern that led to his decision:

I had taken them too far, led them to accept too much and be open to some of the culture's darker sides. I could no longer stand with them. I'm not as liberal as the congregation I had encouraged to develop that way. I found myself less and less comfortable with what was, at least in part, my own creation.

Another pastor confessed:

I never intended that the charismatic movement should go so far in my congregation. It has become the norm of membership and, while I share the experience with my people, I can't identify with those who use it as a form of exclusion.

The members of a congregation also know the feeling of theological dis-identification. "I don't know what has happened," one lay leader exclaimed. "Ever since Jim came here three years ago we've been less and less a house of prayer and more and more a political platform."

There is always likely to be a healthy challenge to the theological positions of both pastor and congregation in a vital, searching and faithful church. But the time between pastors, as we shall see, is a good time for a congregation to reflect on its theology and work at making changes which will yield energy and harmony within the body.

Selective Dis-identification

There are many examples of the ways in which both pastor and parishioner detach themselves from certain segments of the congregation's life and program or parts of the responsibilities and activities of leadership. In this case, portions of the church's life are left unattended, or at least, ill-attended, i.e., the pastoral work related to Christian education, outreach, evangelism, stewardship, worship, pastoral visitation or advocacy. The failure to identify with the responsibilities attached to any of these aspects of the church's life may not necessarily be a sign of a preparedness to leave the ministry of that church. However, if the dis-identification is prolonged, members of the congregation who give high priority to particular aspects of the ministry become deeply dissatisfied and disappointed.

It works both ways. There are pastors whose hearts have been broken by congregations who seem to disregard certain aspects of the ministry of the church and are careless of the need to hold all parts of the body in valued trust.

The activities or inactivities that result from dis-identification lead to various levels of disorganization when a pastor is leaving. Such signs of endings, however, may be distant early warnings for those who care about the organization of the church and who want to assure its continuity and renewal.

CHAPTER 3

Disorganization

Some questions were asked of pastors in a transition workshop just before they left their churches to take up new pastoral appointments:

—When did you stop long range planning?

—When did you decide it would be all right simply to repeat some things you had been quite creative in doing before?

—When did it become less important to encourage that committee or this chairperson about a new initiative?

Their responses indicated a direct correlation between the timing of these changes in behavior, and the time (usually one to five months) before they decided to move. Such changes in a pastor's enthusiasm and intensity go unnoticed at first by most of the congregation, but a few people get distant early warning signals which indicate that an attitudinal change has taken place and that a part of the organization is suffering.

In our study of the things that impede progress of effective congregational mission planning, at least half the factors relate to the disorganization that results from the pastor being "in another place" from that of most of his or her congregation. The "other place" may be defined theologically, socially, subjectively and/or professionally, but the result is the same—varying levels of disorganization.

When the congregation enters the next stage of its corporate life cycle—a new building, a new direction for ministry, a new level of viewing the world for purposes of mission focus—direct, intentional leadership is required. If the pastor is thinking about moving, the energy and enthusiasm to work at creating the commitments for growth and change are difficult to muster. Pastors feel guilty about leading people to new levels of commitment when they are sensing reduced levels themselves. It is especially true in matters related to budget and expensive programs.

One pastor put it this way:

> My first clue to my own attitude came when I heard myself saying that I was not prepared to develop a new program for mission education until I was sure we could afford the projects that might be inspired by that program. That was not like me! Normally I would have recognized that the congregation would itself decide on the relative merits and feasibility of program and project options. My job was to inspire, engage and interpret. I had become more concerned to conserve and retrench and it was probably a result of the fact that I didn't want to leave a debt load behind.

This cautious attitude can also be seen in lay leaders. The insecurity of the job market has led to an attitude in many congregations that is both conservative and even regressive. Since many of the leading members in congregations spend much of their energy wondering how long they will be where they are, there is less energy and initiative for careful planning, growth development and outreach. An organization that has traditional ways of working, planning and deciding begins to get mixed messages from the pastor and/or lay leaders.

Care should be taken not to assume that disorganization is only the result of a lack of security of place and future. Disorientation or disorganization is related to dis-identification as well.

One lay leader, commenting on the apparent hints of disorganization that revealed a pastor's intention to move, made this important link:

> I noticed he was missing meetings without letting us know in advance. There was an obvious lack of preparation and a loss of interest and enthusiasm with the issues that were facing us. This went on for nearly six months before he actually announced he was leaving.

Part of that behavior was, no doubt, a result of the pastor's new agendas. These led to activities more concerned with the future than with the organizational needs of the present.

Types of Disorganization

Three forms of disorganization have been discerned. First, there are obvious kinds of *personal disorganization* when a pastor is leaving.

In addition to the behavior that results from displaced loyalties and interests there is the distraction which betrays a waning sense of responsibility for the future.

Second, when the announcement to leave has been made, another form of disorganization takes effect, this time in the committees and boards of the church. *Structural disorganization* can be seen in statements like the following which were overheard in a church where the pastor was leaving:

—We shouldn't make this decision until the new pastor comes.

—We had better not get this started until we know what kind of commitment our new pastor will have to the idea.

—This was really our former pastor's concern and we probably won't follow through on it now that he is leaving.

These statements belie ownership of committee projects and goals. It becomes obvious that, in spite of what may have been said, there is a heavy dependency upon the pastor for inspiration, support, and leadership.

The third type of disorganization is in the realm of staff roles, functions, and loyalties. *Staff disorganization* is most marked in churches with a number of fulltime staff. The phenomenon called "the changing hole" is known to many people. This alludes to the fact that when a pastor is leaving, the remaining staff members often shift their work load and sense of responsibility in such a way that they fill the hole caused by the departure. There are times when, if the vacancy goes on for an extended period, the work, roles and pastoral identities of the one who has left are subsumed by others. The person called to replace a former pastor then finds it difficult to find the "hole" that was left. Pastoral relations committees, "call" committees and others charged with the responsibility of orienting candidates to the role, find that what they described to the applicants may in fact no longer be the place of need by the time a new pastor arrives. When this happens there is danger of disillusionment or disappointment either on the part of congregation or pastor because what was, is present no longer, and what was described as the vacancy does not appear to exist. This situation can lead to some conflict or struggle between an incoming pastor and those who are the continuing staff. Congregations must make intentional decisions about whether to hold the "hole" open, using interim ministers or selected lay leaders, or let the staff renegotiate its ministry roles before a new pastor is called.

Normal concerns about the relationships that will change and the questions about the ability of various staff members to accommodate to the coming "mysterious new person" all require planning and attention.

Disorganization and Disenchantment

Sometimes a form of disorganization precipitates a pastoral change. Pastors report that there is a high level of frustration with congregations that make decisions at one level of the church's structure but fail either to set in place infrastructure for administering their decisions or, having such infrastructure in place, fail to contribute the necessary volunteer leadership. Others indicate that disorganization occurs when too many people feel they have the right or responsibility to change or re-do committee and board work. When promises once made are rescinded, initiatives embarked on are later abandoned, and idealism (masquerading as resolve) leads to careless policy making or unplanned mission designs, pastors can become seriously disillusioned. These feelings can be the fundamental cause of disenchantment leading to a decision to move.

In some cases at least, the announcement that a pastor is leaving, leads to a more careful lay administrative focus and increased ownership, by lay leaders, of the decisions taken and the plans made.

Oscillation: a Cause

One of the major factors in disorganization at the time of a pastoral change may be related to a phenomenon described by Bruce Reed[1] as "oscillation." Reed indicates that within each of us there is the need to move alternately between a condition of intra-dependence and one of extra-dependence. His research suggests that we oscillate between believing, on the one hand, that our self-confirmation, protection and sustenance is a matter within our own control, (intra-dependence) to believing that it is a matter that depends on a person or object other than ourselves (extra-dependence). Both religious and secular activities provide the environment in which this oscillation takes place.

In broad terms, those who are in a state of intra-dependence can take for granted the aims and values they bring to activities and can therefore participate with a sense of energy and confidence. Reed suggests that people in intra-dependence are tolerant of uncertainty and ambiguity and are not particularly disturbed by anxiety. By contrast those in extra-dependence find uncertainties and

---

[1]Bruce Reed, *Dynamics of Religion* (London: Darton, Dongman and Todd, 1978).

anxieties intolerable and express feelings of "self-doubt, confusion, fatigue, guilt and weakness." (Reed, p. 90)

As individuals oscillate from one condition to the other it changes the way in which they participate in and respond to the ministry of the church. Those expressing intra-dependence have energy and commitment, a well-spring of faith resources, high motivation and inner-urgings toward participation, action and service within the congregation and the world. Those expressing extra-dependence on the other hand, need the church to serve them, nourish their fading commitments and encourage their waning faith. In extra-dependence the church is a resource. In intra-dependence the church can be a means through which persons express themselves in ministry.

What causes the shift or oscillation from one side to the other may be very personal experiences: daily or weekly rhythms, changes in jobs, status, relationships, and levels of security. Because of these shifts it is clear that members of congregations have, intermittently, to call upon the church for different kinds of services, and will participate in different ways.

These shifting needs and responses seem to accelerate or become more pronounced in congregations undergoing pastoral change. The phenomenon of oscillation has direct application also in the life of the pastor and the pastor's family.

When a pastor leaves, some members who have been deeply involved in sharing, contributing and expressing their gifts of leadership in the work of ministry choose that time to move to the other side. They want to assume that relationship in which the church, its worship, music, program and staff, serve them rather than vice versa. It is difficult for them to do that while the pastor is in place. They don't want to let him or her down, nor do they want to reflect negatively on what is being done or jeopardize the relationship between pastor and people. With the announcement that the pastor is leaving, however, many people feel freer to let go of initiatives and leadership functions.

Conversely, some people who have been enjoying the service of the church have been strengthened, healed and encouraged by its ministry. They may choose this time to oscillate into a more assertive and intentional form of active membership. It is notable, for instance, that many congregations are surprised that some folks who have not appeared to be deeply involved will let it be known that they would like to take some responsibility just as a pastor is leaving or before the new pastor comes.

All of this can be both troubling and confusing for the pastor who is preparing to leave, as it becomes obvious that a significant shift in lay leadership is taking place. Those who know the importance of the work of the nominating committee to the general tone and program strength of the congregation, frequently feel deep levels of concern about the shifts that take place. The transfer of leadership has been described by some pastors as something like a *coup d'etat*. Timing is a factor in this process. Because most congregations have their annual meeting in January the officers are elected at that time. If that work is completed before the pastor announces his or her decision to leave, i.e., by February or March, then the effect of oscillation is not as evident as it is when the pastor announces a decision to leave in October or November before the congregational nominating committee has finished its work.

Some of this should not surprise or trouble us. It is a normal outgrowth of the oscillation which all of us feel from time to time and which is easier to act upon in the period "between pastors." Some feel, as one lay leader put it, "If I bow out before the new pastor comes, it won't appear to be a reflection on him."

Part of the difficulty with this process is that much of it is unconscious, often it is misinterpreted, and frequently inappropriate motives are suspected. In fact in the work done by Roy Oswald[2] and others on leader burn-out it has been found that congregations need to allow lay leaders to oscillate within the congregation. Otherwise, and this is frequently the case—strong active lay leaders who wish to spend some time having a rest from church commitments find that they have to go somewhere else to escape the pressure of assignments, assumptions and expectations.

Pastors oscillate too. In fact one of the major reasons for pastoral changes is related to the need for a pastor to change direction. Some feel the need to move into a relationship where the strength of the congregation will nurture and refresh a tired and hurt leader. Others want to get to a place where their skills, gifts and knowledge will be used in a more interesting and challenging way.

But all of that is hard to describe in terms that will neither hurt nor demean the people with whom the pastor has worked, grown and matured. It seems almost unforgivable to feel, as many pastors do, that the three or four years in their congregation have been such a positive experience which strengthened and refreshed their spirit, that now they are ready to take on a new challenge, greater responsibility and a more complex mininstry—but want to go somewhere else to do it. Only a wider perspective relieves the feeling of guilt.

---

[2]Roy Oswald, *Clergy Burnout: A Survival Kit for Church Professionals.*

Dealing with Disorganization

We need to see a pastoral career on a larger time line, and the nature of the relationship between congregation and clergy on a broader plane to see the justice in that situation. We need also to recognize that much of what causes weakness, need, pain and anxiety in pastors is not related to a particular congregation. There are family relationships, aspects of life style, the effect of aging, and feelings of disenchantment that have more to do with the culture than with the church.

All of these conditions contribute to the pastor's need to be with people who basically understand his or her situation and who can be a source of encouragement and healing. Of course pastors are encouraged to find people in every stage of their lives who can be a support and strength. However, sometimes only a complete change of parish will be sufficient to allow the freedom for personal change.

The opposite is true also. There are pastors who come to the deep conviction that the relationships they have developed and the congregation that has settled in with them are so comfortable as to dampen the prophetic fires that give meaning to preaching and teaching. Then a move seems necessary. It provides the catalytic effect that frees intra-dependent responses and activities, and calls on the gifts and skills to make them vibrant and alive again.

Having explored the many types of dis-identification, it is of little surprise that misunderstanding can arise at the time of pastoral change. Once again, healthy, open discussion of these experiences is encouraged. The pastor and key lay leaders may help a congregation immeasurably by assisting as these various causes and symptoms are recognized and clarified.

CHAPTER 4

Disengagement

Sometimes a pastor has most difficulty in answering the question "Why are you leaving?" When it comes to the time of disengagement. There is work attached to each level of activity in disengagement and the emotional and physical strain can be heavy.

How pastors and congregations handle the processes of leave taking is, in many ways, a mark of their maturity and a sign of the quality of their relationships.

Others have explored the process of pastoral change in terms of grief and its related emotions. It may be useful to note the various levels of relationship that need attention at this transition time.

The Process

Each denomination has its polity concerning leave taking. Some is written, much of it is in the realm of oral tradition. It is important to know what is expected both by congregation and pastor at the time of disengagement. All formal arrangements should be carefully discussed and agreed upon as early as possible. It is important to ask and have answers for the questions concerning obligations of the members of the congregation to the departing pastor and his or her family. Without knowing what is expected, the congregation cannot enjoy the opportunity to do the unexpected.

Schedules of final commitments and opportunities for shared labor, if known and invited, can be occasions for both formal and informal leave-taking rituals. All elements of the process can hold potential for misunderstanding, embarrassment and even deep hurt. Some forethought will be helpful.

Relationships

It seems a simple thing, but it is important to some people to have been told about a pending resignation in confidence, before the

general announcement is made. The feelings of those who have
worked most closely with the pastor, who may be the most deeply
and emotionally affected by his or her departure and/or those who
have a right to know because of their place in the organization,
need to be considered. This is however also open to misunderstanding. There are bound to be some who will think they should
be considered to be in "the inner circle."

It is as much the responsibility of the lay leaders of a congregation as of the pastor to care for the hurt feelings of those who discover they were not consulted or informed. The task is just too
complicated for any one person to do successfully. Certainly, the
denominational officials most directly related to the church and pastor should be carefully informed and briefed.

Perhaps, more important than the question of *who* is informed
about a decision to move, are those questions related to the *how*
and *why* of the announcement. Most pastors find it wise to adhere
to the traditional denominational patterns, and a clear, deliberate
and explanatory announcement can dispel rumors, erase wounds
and facilitate the healthy handling of grief.

Unfortunately some pastors play games at this point in the process, and such games are unbecoming to a professional. Some of
the games are called:

—God made me do it.

—I'd really like to stay, but. . . .

—It's the Bishop's fault.

—Nobody knows the trouble I've seen. . . .

—I can't help it if I'm so much in demand.

Far more authentic expressions of the levels of feeling and attitudes
are usually well-received and appreciated at this time.

In any congregation there are many women and men who have
been through vocational and career transitions—some many
times—and will therefore react to inappropriate behavior on the
part of the pastor. This can have the effect of destroying the credi-
bility which has taken years to establish. Pastors who play their
departure announcement for its dramatic and shock value belie a
pastoral concern and deny their fundamental relationships with the
colleagues with whom they have had a trusting association.

A carefully worded and well-articulated statement, agreed upon
by officials responsible for the ongoing stability of the congregation
and the departing pastor, can dispel doubt and deflect difficulties

related to the future expectations. Such a statement can also ward off embarrassing invitations which often follow a minister's departure.

Disengagement is most difficult when there has been dispute, conflict, disappointment or outright confrontation that precipitates the decision to leave. When any of these conditions apply, it is quite appropriate for a congregation to seek assistance from a consultant—preferably one with experience in congregational transitions. Many of the feelings within a congregation will haunt the future if not allowed expression, interpretation and response.

A Good Goodbye

At the farewell gathering for one pastor and his family, a number of important things were said which provide a thought-provoking outline for the consideration of issues related to disengagement:

You will be missed!

To acknowledge loss and grief is not only helpful, but therapeutic. Frequently the changing of pastors marks important passages in the lives of people in a congregation. There have been significant times shared and special events in the lives of some people, which were deepened by the ministry of the person leaving.

Sometimes, members of the pastor's family have played vital roles in the life of a congregation and the loss of these valued relationships will be felt deeply. They will need to be articulated.

There will always be a place for you here, but it will not be the same place.

While pastors are not encouraged to return officially to churches they have served, it is important to acknowledge that they are welcome to maintain the important connections of friendship and concern that have marked their stay.

A clear statement made by a natural leader in the congregation at the time of disengagement can be most helpful. The distinction can be drawn between the appropriateness of returning as a friend—one who has shared the journey, and even led the sojourners for a time—rather than as a participant in the ministerial life of the congregation.

One such statement was pointed but yet welcoming:

There may be times when our future pastors invite you to share their ministry with them. When they invite you, we will be most delighted to welcome you.

Such a definition of authority is helpful and freeing, both at the time it is stated and later when guidance and care is needed.

We expect to grow and change because of the roots you have planted and the confidence we have gained while you were here.

It is both comforting and freeing for a pastor to be told that things will change and flourish after he or she leaves. From the congregational point of view it helps people to interpret the changes that will come, but at the same time discourages interference from the former pastor in the future development of the church.

Many who wish to resist change in a congregation find a willing ally in the former pastor. After all, the pastor and people worked to establish things as they are now. To those who are not open to change, any form of change seems like a negative reflection on what was done in the past.

At the time of disengagement some important steps can be taken to anticipate development and change and remove the potential for future tensions:

Because of your ministry with us, we know the value of a pastor's presence. . .and so we will be replacing you, just as you will be replacing someone else.

This is another reminder that an ending has taken place. The first part of that sentence may well be embellished on the basis of the facts of the strong and significant relationships and work that mark the ministry of the past. The latter part of the sentence specifically acknowledges the reality of transition.

Since the Church of Jesus Christ is bigger than any one local expression of it, we can rest assured that the good work you do elsewhere will be appreciated by us, and the good work we do will strengthen you.

It is tempting at the time of disengagement, to focus on the work and ministry of a single person in a single place. The doctrine of the church is elevated, however, when those who may be tempted to a myopic view of the value of the pastor's ministry, are reminded that it is possible to share that ministry within a wider context. A statement that acknowledges the relationship between churches some distance from one another has a particular poignancy at the time of disengagement. The connectionalism within the church is made possible when friends, pastors and associates move away from one another taking with them the assurance that "we are one in the spirit," and "united in Christ."

No one knows when endings begin. For some it could be said that their ministry in a given place never really got started. To speak of endings in that case seems irrelevant, but in fact may be even more relevant than could be at first recognized. Some churches, deeply grieving the loss of a beloved pastor and pastor's family never really adapt to the new one. In these cases some pastors begin a new ministry without realizing that it is probably an interim. Some pastors grieving the loss of a former congregational relationship where needs were met, challenges accepted, goals attended to and visions and dreams expanded never quite embrace a new one.

Short, stormy and often conflictual pastoral relationships can often be seen as the result of the failure of church or pastor or both to look after the work of their endings.

In the Interim

CHAPTER 5

A Significant Interval

Just as it is difficult to know when endings begin, it is also not clear when the time between pastors starts and ends. The most obvious way to measure it is to think in terms of the physical presence, or absence, of a pastor, but in fact that does not reflect the important subtlety of the situation.

The congregational members actually begin to feel they are "between pastors" when the signs and feelings of *endings* are experienced. Certainly, from the time a formal announcement is made indicating a pastor's decision to leave, a number of the elements of the interim period begin to take effect. The interim is an interval between the process of endings and the process of beginnings, but there is clearly an overlap. This allows for some very significant work to be done, both by the pastor who is leaving and the lay leaders of the congregation.

Possibilities and Problems

Many congregations seek assistance to use the time between pastors effectively.

Some call in consultants to assist them to anticipate, deal with and even utilize the feelings of endings. Others have come to value wise counsel from denominational staff people, or well-trained interim ministers as they make the necessary adjustments to the new situation caused by the departure of a pastor. Still others have found resources from within the congregation itself to bridge successfully the gap between pastors.

Loren Mead of The Alban Institute believes that this time can be a "prime time for renewal."[1] His experience shows that such an

---

[1] The Alban Institute (Washington, DC) produced a package in 1977 which included audio cassette, filmstrip and print material for churches in the midst of pastoral change. *Prime Time for Renewal* is the title of the package and of the

interim provides both time and opportunity for lay leaders of the
church to search out their own authentic understanding of the ministry and become intentional about the lay leadership functions of
congregational life.

Not everyone agrees! Some feel that the pastor is such an inte-
gral part of the fabric of the church's ministry, that a prolonged
period without a resident clergyperson would be detrimental to the
ongoing strength of congregational vitality. For many, the pastor is a
symbol of the stability and continuity of the dispersed people of
God. Without that symbol, these people believe the forces which
always lurk near the edges of Christian commitment would have a
detrimental effect upon the congregational vision and direction.

Some denominational systems allow for, and even encourage,
the use of interim pastors. Others tend to leave little or no time
between pastoral ministries, thus assuring a sense of security and
continuity in the local congregation.

Rather than argue for or against a particular system, it seems
more important to recognize that an interim period *does* take place
even in those churches where the new pastor is installed the week
after the former pastor leaves. The interim actually begins when the
signs of endings become evident. That can be, and often is, months
before the actual leave-taking or disengagement. The interim stage
continues well into the first few months of a new pastor's ministry
and until he or she is identified with, and accepted by, the receiving
congregation. The importance of this interim time has been well
expressed by a denominational officer in addressing a "vacant" congregation:

> This could be a most significant time for your congregation. It is
> a time when you can review the past with its symbols and
> images of identity and purpose as well as its losses and disap-
> pointments. You can allow yourself time to feel those losses and
> the elements of leadership that are sure to follow along an effec-
> tive ministry. You can also begin to value the strengths and gifts
> of people in the congregation who step up now to offer leader-
> ship, knowing that, with the loss of a significant leader, others
> will be called upon to provide wisdom and guidance. You can
> begin to glimpse new opportunities made possible because of

book by William A. Yon. More recently (1986) a book, *Critical Moment of Ministry:
A Change of Pastors*, by Loren Mead was published by The Alban Institute and now
accompanies a video tape produced in cooperation with the Centre for Study of
Church and Ministry. The video and print package is entitled *So Your Pastor's Leaving*.

the fact that your pastor has left. Above all, as a congregation, you can take responsibility for identifying new directions for your church's ministry, a new vision for your church's mission and a "grassroots" definition of the church's purpose. This is, and has always been *your* church. Your former pastor believed that and sought to serve your mutual understandings. If the new pastor is to do the same it will be necessary for you as a congregation to clarify your own church's mission.

But can this happen? What steps and activities are needed and what organization of tasks will facilitate such an optimistic outcome?

Planning for the interim period and sharing the plan with as many of the church's members as possible creates a helpful environment in which change can take place. It will also serve the congregation well to be deliberate and intentional about arranging for appropriate settings to undertake the work during this time. The result of the interim work, when shared with a new pastor, will provide a basis for deep and rich dialogue about the shared commitments to be made and the mutual ministry to be undertaken.

Identifying the Losses

When a pastor leaves a congregation there is always a variety of feelings of loss. This is true whether the relationship between pastor and congregation has been satisfying and vital or not.

Personal Losses

For those whose faith journey has been made clearer or stronger because of a pastor's leadership, a certain sense of anxiety and even abandonment emerges in the absence of that significant person. For those who valued the pastoral care and nurture provided by the former pastor during critical or particularly difficult times, the sense of loss resembles that of the removal of a member of the family.

Some people describe their feelings as "a loss of a colleague." Those who have shared the work of ministry, the commitments and the intensity of Christian action, the struggle for clarity of vision have developed a working relationship with the pastor. This will feel weakened or even threatened by the departure of one with whom they have experienced so much.

For a few people the feelings of loss are related to the fact that they shared a certain spiritual space, the common bond of deep devotion, which is difficult enough to establish and quite unlikely to

be replicated, at least for some time. Longer pastorates tend to fos-
ter these deep bonds of spiritual understanding which make leave-
taking difficult for a pastor, since he or she cannot be sure of find-
ing such a supportive and rewarding relationship somewhere else.
Because soul partnership is rare, many who have developed that
symbiotic spiritual link with their pastor may indeed be expressing
a deep truth when they say, "It will never be the same."

For others, of course, a loss of a pastor is not a major cause of
grief. Even for active members in many congregations, the experience of pastoral change has been frequent enough that they have
avoided getting too close to the pastor thus protecting their own
emotions. Pastors, too, may keep a certain emotional distance knowing that their stay will not be many years in duration and that for
them, leave-taking would engender a number of mixed feelings.

Grief is experienced in proportion to the levels of feeling
involved in the elements of endings. For those seriously disenchanted, leave-taking is experienced as release. If they have developed
high levels of dis-identification, leaving is an opportunity for a new
identification. If in the period before the pastor leaves, the church
has experienced much confusion of leadership or disorganization,
the end of a ministry can be seen as an opportunity to reorganize.

Where there has been conflict, hurt and continuing disagree-
ment between clergy and laity prior to a pastor's leaving, the actual
disengagement can bring times of remorse, feelings of guilt and
even some effort at last minute reconciliation. Where some people
in a congregation are believed to have created the conditions that
led to the decision to leave, there will be other feelings of loss: the
loss of harmony, and of unity with the church body.

Providing the means by which members and friends of the congregation can identify, acknowledge and articulate the many levels
of personal loss felt at the time of a pastoral change can be of
immense value. A forum where permission is given to recognize
and name the many faces of loss will assist in preparing the ground
for an open new relationship between pastor and congregation.
Unacknowledged grief is often expressed in ways that are both irrational and unmanageable. Such expressions may lead to strained
relationship between members of a congregation on the one hand,
or between the new pastor and his or her new congregation on the
other. Frequently, grief is expressed in ways that are hurtful or
debilitating for a new pastor/parish relationship. It is unfortunate
that those most directly affected are often unable to recognize the
source or understand the intensity of the feelings.

Pastors also must deal with their own sense of loss. Unless this
happens they may move to a new pastoral charge unable to begin

the process of engagement with a sense of openness and freedom that makes such activity helpful and healthy.

For pastors and their families, levels of grief vary, depending on the depth of shared commitments and values, the richness of the mutual engagement with the former ministry and mission and their satisfaction with the levels of support and common understandings of faith.

Pastors can be caught in their own mixed motives at the time of endings. They are disturbed by the intermingled feelings of loss, guilt, anxiety, exhilaration and anticipation. Such confusion of feeling sometimes leads to unusual behavior which may both surprise and upset members of the congregation. Pastors, who send mixed messages as to the reasons for leaving, or who seem to magnify petty grievances out of proportion, may be simply reacting adversely as a way of coping with all the entwined feelings of loss and hope.

One pastor, in retrospect, was able to sort out her feelings and, at least in part, explain her unusual behavior in the last weeks of her ministry in a small rural charge. She said:

> I really was happy to be leaving a small town. I'd felt stifled there but I realized that it was nobody's fault but my own. I'd carried a bias with me into that community and no matter what those people did I wouldn't let them close to me. They wanted to organize a big farewell and I frustrated those who were planning it. I think I was afraid they would really get to me and I would have to admit there was no good reason for my leaving except that I wanted a bigger church and higher profile in the denomination. I often wish I could go back and do a better job of saying "goodbye."

Both pastors and lay leaders need permission to own their grief and name their losses.

Organizational losses

Besides personal losses, congregations can feel a deep sense of organizational confusion and structural insecurity during the interim period. In spite of well-intended and idealistic talk about the concept of mutual ministry and shared leadership, the fact is there is always a unique role played by a clergyperson in the work of planning and administration in most churches. His or her leaving then, tends to destabilize the organization and administration of a congregation. Without some careful counsel, congregations may not realize how complex the interdependency between pastor and congregation has become.

In the matter of leadership initiative alone a major disequilibrium results from the departure of a pastor. The extent of the disruption, of course, depends on the experience and assumptions of those who are left to continue the work of ministry.

Roy Oswald has used a helpful diagram to show varying levels of inter-dependency between pastor and lay leader.[2] A similar diagram (below) shows, graphically different ways in which pastors and parishioners work out a stable relationship around leadership initiative.

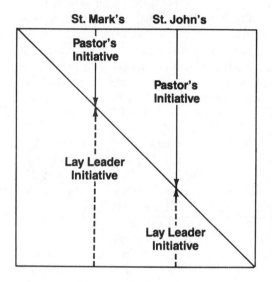

At St. John's the assumption is that much of the leadership initiative will come from the pastor; the lay leaders will be supportive and helpful. At St. Mark's, on the other hand, the roles are reversed with most of the initiative coming from lay leaders who enjoy the support of the enabling ministry of their pastor. Both churches may well be quite satisfied with their customary relationship. However if, for some reason, the pastors were to change places, both would feel considerable organizational loss. Disorganization in a congregation at the time of pastoral change is most marked where the history of the leadership initiative has been biased toward the pastor. Since we will return to the concept of changing leadership initiative ratios later in addressing the work of "New Beginnings," it is suffi-

---

[2]Roy M. Oswald, *The Pastor as Newcomer* (Washington, DC: The Alban Institute, 1977), 2.

cient to point out here that whatever the leadership style and ratio arrived at in pastor/parish relationships, it will be destabilized with the departure of the pastor.

Loss of Momentum

One of the most marked signs of organizational loss in congregations experiencing pastoral change is in the realm of *momentum*. Frequently, the energy given to developing future directions and clarifying goals and objectives wanes both in the pastor and in key lay leaders when it is known that the pastor intends to leave, so programs that benefit from joint enthusiasm may suffer a loss of momentum while a congregation awaits a new minister's leadership. Individuals who have been eager to share the work of ministry with their pastor often lose interest when their relationship is broken as a result of a move.

Committees that are responsible for the work that relied on the skills of the pastor may feel discouraged and even deceived by the announcement that the pastor is going to work somewhere else. The resulting loss of identification with the committee work is debilitating. Resignations from committees, the withdrawal of financial support, absenteeism on the part of committee and board members, and a distinct loss of energy toward long and short range planning can all result from the announcement of a pastor's resignation. All these contribute to organizational loss.

Loss of Confidence and Trust

"It seems we just nicely got started with a capable pastor working well with our committees and then the cabinet decided to move him." This expression of a lay leader identifies another kind of loss that may be felt at the news of a pending pastoral change. It is the loss of confidence in the system that appoints pastors.

What is even worse is the nagging feeling of many people, that the pastor probably suggested that it was time for a move, or at least acquiesced too easily in the call of the denominational executive to go elsewhere. Either way the congregation feels it has been the loser. Anger and frustration can lead to unfortunate barrier-building between the congregation and the uninvolved new pastor. When this happens, the congregation may distrust the denominational executive and the system that seems to be the source of their grief and pain.

In churches with a "call" system it is usually clear that the pastor has decided that a pastoral change is in order. It is not so clear in an "appointive" system and the feelings of loss are not always given opportunity for expression.

When a pastor leaves there is, for a few people in the congregation, a loss of vision or hope, since the pastor has symbolized that for some and articulated it for others. An opportunity to express that loss, and to identify with others who feel it, can prevent displacement and the quiet discouragement of those who have been most dependent upon pastoral leadership. For those who are not dependent, but who feel strongly aligned with their pastor's vision or image of the church, news of a resignation can be cause for alienation and antagonism toward the church that reappoints or calls pastors away. A careful handling of both the explanation for change and the feelings that result from the experience is vital to the smooth transfer of pastoral leadership.

Pastors who are less than honest about their motives and the part they play in denominational decision-making fail in one of their final acts of ministry by contributing to a loss of respect for denominational leadership and the loss of confidence in the wider church.

Assessing the New Situation

A pastoral change is an opportunity for the congregation to restructure priorities in ministry, to renew skills and knowledge through the person of a new leader, and to reinterpret the goals and objectives of the church's ministry. All of this may be accomplished without reflecting prejudicially on the priorities, skills and interpretations provided by the former pastor. Unfortunately, however, both new pastors and members frequently succumb to the temptation to gain strength for their arguments for change by unfavorable comparison with the past. This behavior usually betrays the trust that has been developed in former relationships and also proves to be counter-productive. It tends to encourage people to dwell on the past and can deflect the energy needed for the future.

Restructuring Priorities

Congregational priorities usually shift as a result of the mutual assimilation of values and concerns of both clergy and laity. Those priorities that challenge a congregation at any given time are neither purely the reflection of the collective mind of the laity, nor of the clergy leadership. Clergy can influence the specific emphasis that will prevail when priorities are being set, but if that influence becomes oppressive or untenable, lay leaders have ways of righting the balance.

When a pastor leaves, however, there is an opportunity to assess the degree to which the priorities, expressed in program and budget, reflect those of a congregation as it now exists. It may well be that such a reassessment of priorities should take place before negotiations with a new pastor conclude in order that the understandings arrived at by a new pastor and congregation are faithful to the deepest sense of concern and commitment of the membership. A lifelong member of one church gives us a good example of the way priorities shift:

> When Ken left, we realized that for seventeen years we had been privileged to have been sharing the ministry with a superb pastor and counsellor, a fine teacher and a very special friend. We set out to try to find another like him. However, as we interviewed and especially when we listened to some other ministers *preach*, we began to realize that we would be enriched by a pastor who had strong *preaching* skills. In fact, before we completed our search process, *"preaching ability"* became one of our highest priorities.

Other shifts in priorities have led congregations to become very intentional in their search and negotiation processes. Those shifts can emerge without any derogatory or hurtful critique of former leadership. They simply reflect the congregation's willingness to seize an opportunity to readjust priorities.

If this is done in perfunctory or shallow ways, however, the new priorities may neither reflect the real attitudes of the whole congregation, nor the more careful assessment of the needs of the church and community.

Program priority shifts at times of pastoral change can result in unclear expectations of the new pastor. For this reason, consultants recommend that congregations take time to do an evaluation before the search process gets too near completion. The time between pastors allows for congregational restructuring of mission priorities. It is wise and even productive to use it that way.

Gaining New Skills and Knowledge

"I felt as though I was called to a church that didn't want me." This assessment, after eighteen months of ministry, was probably accurate. Having failed to assess shifts in program and ministry priorities and having left the search for a new pastor to a few of the "old guard," this church called a pastor well suited to their *old* self image, but ill-prepared for the growing new sense of purpose in the majority of new members. Early feelings of alienation had shaken the new pastor's self-confidence and divided the congregation. Unfortunately, the division had led to the formation of groups on either side of the pastor, but the real division in the congregation was on the matter of ministry and mission priorities. Had church leaders been clear about their priorities in the first place, the pastor might well have been able to adjust his leadership initiative to respond.

Conversely, congregations that establish clear guidelines for the nature of the ministry they wish to pursue can seek, in prospective pastoral leadership, the very skills, experience and attitudes which best provide support and inspiration for their goals.

An empty pulpit may be an open invitation to a congregation to become careful and deliberate in assessing the very skills, gifts, graces and levels of experience that will propel them into adventuresome ministries. Such a careful assessment will also facilitate the depth of dialogue between prospective pastors and the church's committees. This allows pastors to accept invitations to congregations where they would be able to work from their strengths.

Practical Help

Materials are available to help congregations to make a more accurate assessment of priorities; their judicious use will facilitate the search and call process.[3] Pastors will need to do a self assessment on the basis of their own priorities, commitments and evaluations prior to their contact with congregations seeking a new minister. Once again, excellent resources are available.

For those who would seek to undertake an assessment with the help of a career counsellor, there are well-located centers with skilled counsellors in North America. Many pastors use these resources without any sense of urgency, feeling neither dissatisfied nor discouraged, but rather desirous of moving "from strength to strength." Since pastors' priorities change from time to time as do those of congregations, many clergy wisely undertake a periodic review of their essential understandings of their work in ministry.

---

[3]One such resource is the *Guide for Congregational Self-Evaluation*, which is available from The Episcopal Church Center, 815 Second Avenue, New York, NY 10017. Another is a *Manual for Pastor-Parish Relations Committees* published by and available from The Center for Parish Development, 1448 53rd Street, Chicago, IL 60615.

Such reassessments prepare them to be more effective and specific in their conversations with prospective congregations. Such reassessments also provide clergy with a sense of confidence in their work, not to mention the increased energy and enthusiasm that comes with the knowledge that they are using the strongest gifts and qualities they possess.

Finding New Directions

Three elements must be considered if a pastor and a congregation are to take seriously the opportunity afforded by this "in between" time in a pastoral change.

Explore the Meaning of History

First, it will be essential to explore the meanings that come out of the past. Congregations benefit from joyful but reflective examination of the past to discover what essential attitudes and assumptions are functioning now as a result of the influences from the past. Images of the church which are drawn from "the good old days" can be so overpowering as to impede any significant attempt to identify future goals, objectives and points of mission. As a result of a prolonged, intentional and well designed process of gaining new perspective on their church's history, a number of congregations have identified fascinating new directions.

One congregation, for example, in reappraising its historical processes of decision making, discovered that too few people had been involved in the identification and shaping of congregational mission and initiatives. While seeing that traditional pattern, the congregation also recognized some of the difficulties they had been meeting in recruiting and enabling the ministry of new lay leaders. In the interim, before a new pastor arrived, the congregation took action to limit the tenure of committee chairpeople, established some guidelines for the introduction of "new members" onto major committees and boards, and intentionally invited some relatively recent arrivals in the congregation to be on the selection committee for the new pastor. All of these actions had the effect of making appreciable change in the structural power of the congregation before the new pastor arrived. This eliminated any possibility of attaching "blame" for such decisive action to the new pastor.

A pastor, who experienced a number of years of frustrating and demoralizing ministry in a congregation that seemed to need skills and abilities he did not possess, accepted a call to be an associate in a church with a multiple staff. For some it seemed like a demotion, but for the intentional pastor it was a carefully planned move to respond to his own self assessment. By becoming an associate, he provided for himself a colleague relationship to overcome a near burn-out condition, and the freedom to concentrate on those aspects of his ministry in which he had always been considered effective.

Both of these positive actions were taken after careful reflection on the lessons of the past.

Analysis of Context

Secondly, churches often continue to function in ways that fit conditions that have not existed for some time in their community. Before a new pastor is introduced to the congregation and its ministry, it seems appropriate to reappraise the context in which the church serves. Again a number of resources are designed to assist congregations in this reappraisal. The use of these can yield helpful and even vital perspectives suggesting new directions for church planning and programming.

One congregation, having undertaken a careful reassessment of its context came to the startling conclusion that "the future of our church is with the elderly." In their analysis of the data concerning their community, members of this congregation had learned that the fastest growing segment of the population was that of men and women over sixty years of age. When the church had moved to that community the fastest growing segment had been those between thirty and forty-five. The church, established to serve the people in a given community, had adjusted when that community changed. It now hears a call to adjust again, this time with programs directed toward the elderly.

The careful assessment, including a congregational profile and community analysis, is invaluable in the start-up activities of a new ministry. Both pastor and congregation will begin their new relationship on surer ground if the descriptions of church and community are clear and faithful to the facts.

Assess Theological Position

The third element in a congregation's effort to discover new directions is theological in nature. The interim is a time to reappraise the theological basis on which the congregation is prepared to build its future. As we shall see, congregations tend to reflect more than one theological, program and social emphasis, but it becomes more helpful if, in the time between pastors, an assessment can be made of the place occupied by the congregation on the theological spectrum. Experience shows that when a pastor leaves, there is often a reordering of theological prerogatives in the life of a congregation, and the theological temperature may change appreciably in the interim.

Pastors too may readjust their theological views between pastorates. Some feel that they have been "pushed out of shape" by the particular strengths of theological persuasion in their former congregation. Indeed some church consultants believe that one of the major reasons for voluntary pastoral change is the opportunity such change provides for clergy to readjust their theological positions or to attempt to find in the new pastoral relationship a congregation that better fits their own theological framework. Unfortunately, few program resources to help congregations and prospective pastors discuss in sufficient depth the theological attitudes, beliefs and images that ultimately form the basis of the relationship between them.

However, pastors who lead Bible-study sessions with a significant number of their congregation are in a much stronger position to make such assessments, as are the people who take part.

Identifying Collective Vision: A Process

There a number of ways which have been found to help congregations identify the depth of vision they share. One such exercise projects four possible ways of understanding the role and function of the church: worship and celebration, learning and nurture, support and service, and advocacy.[4] Participants are invited to identify their assessment of the attitudes of the congregation as a whole and then to identify their own specific understanding. A comparison is made. Then participants are invited to designate where, in the future, they would like to see new energy and effort directed. It is explained that through increased commitment, leadership and program activity the "good" of the past need not be lost, but some new effort at increased vision and purpose may be added. Inevitably some patterns emerge providing, at very least, the basis for healthy dialogue around corporate vision and direction. The use of this type of resource is appropriate during the time between pastors. This reflective process allows for the preparation of congregational leaders for significant shifts in the church's focus and energy.

---

[4]Guidelines for leading a congregation through this process, and full description of these categories, are available from the Centre for Study of Church and Ministry, 6000 Iona Drive, Vancouver, BC, Canada V6T 1L4.

Summary

The time between pastors—even the time between the announcement that one is leaving and the first four to six months of a new
pastor's ministry—can be a fruitful and valuable time for a congregation. It allows for purposeful assessment of the depths and
dimensions of loss felt by individual members, committees and
boards. It also allows the pastor to measure his or her similar feelings. It provides for some deliberate activity giving permission for
grief work and for the articulation of the feelings which if unstated,
may impede progress toward the establishment of strong new relationships with future leadership.

The interim period is also a time when the leaders of a congregation can begin to recognize the potential for change, and the
opportunities available to them for gaining the strengths and
insights of another qualified and gifted person. To prepare for the
careful selection of such a person, congregations are encouraged to
assess both the conditioning of the past and the opportunities
raised by the contexts in which the church seeks to do its ministry.
A theological reflection process will assist in predicting the "fit"
between congregation and new pastor.

Finally, as preparation for a new episode in ministry, the congregation is well advised to undertake one of the many procedures that
have been developed to assist members to identify significant new
directions and the emphasis they desire for the future. With such a
preparation the congregation and its chosen pastoral leaders are
poised to engage in the challenging new chapter of work together.

New Beginnings

CHAPTER 6

The Process of Beginning

It's a long step from one church to another. It is more than a moving van away. It is, in significant ways, like a move from one distinct old neighborhood to another distinct old neighborhood. It is not possible to transfer everything that was learned in the one into the other, neither is it likely that the way of being in one will be quite acceptable in the next. There are reasons.

An Analogy

Being called into a new pastoral ministry is a little like being asked to take over from a night school teacher who has already taught the first part of the course.

The students in a night school class know how much time and commitment they intend to give. This is, after all, not the only thing they do. Most of them have full-time jobs, families, homes and other responsibilities, all of which take time and energy and may well demand a higher priority in their lives than does the evening school course. This is true even if the course is a highly significant one.

The class has probably worked out a satisfactory accommodation between course requirements and their individual needs and objectives. The stated and unstated relationships with the teacher about expectations, the meaning of fulfillment and the processes that best serve both person and programs have been clarified.

The members of the class know each other. They are aware of some of the strengths, weaknesses and ideologies of those around them and they have developed an *esprit de corps*. This has emerged as a result as a result of shared experiences and the combined labor of solving problems. They also share the satisfaction derived from being on a common journey. In short, they have a history and a little tradition. The new teacher will discover that the class has a personality which is somewhat dependent upon the experiences that each member brings to it. The collective personality is also a result of the special interplay between time, effort, expectations, the "fit" between persons and the emerging identity that evolves as the class continues to meet. All of this becomes more than the sum of the personal identities of those who make up the student body.

The new teacher also has a personality which reflects a well developed identity. She has an idea about what constitutes a valid and significant course, but doesn't know how much of it has already been taught, let alone how much has been learned.

The new teacher will not understand the inside humor, cannot anticipate the particular accommodation between student commitment and course requirement, and does not really have authority to demand a change in whatever has been established.

There are bound to be adverse comparisons with the former teacher and some strong emotional ties which will result in attitudes and behavior that seem at first irrational. On the other hand, there will probably be some students in the class who welcome and accept the new teacher simply as a well needed change, and as an expression of their hope for a better relationship than they had experienced with the former teacher.

When a new teacher arrives it is as if everything happens at once. There are physical changes, emotional strains, times of testing and opportunities to explore and make mistakes. There are things said that later will be regretted and things not said that would have been helpful. All the communication filters are at work. Images get in the way and so does language. Defenses are up and cross-purposes collide. No one is sure how to proceed. Being called into a new ministry is like that. And there is more. There is the added hope that somehow this relationship between pastor and people will last long enough for both to become instruments of grace in the lives of the other. And indeed, that they each will be vital to the spiritual awakening, journeying and security of the other. The miracle is that it happens—and so often!

Reversing the Process of Endings

To begin a new ministry effectively, both pastor and congregation will need to find ways to reverse the process of endings. Where there was disengagement, the work of beginnings will involve intentional engagement in the search for a harmony of perspective, a level of comfort in working relationships and a blending of gifts and graces.

Where dis-identification marked the weeks and months of endings in the former relationship, the congregation will join the new pastor in focusing their energy on understanding each other's personalities and, eventually, each other's priorities for ministry and mission. Such a focus forges a new, common identity.

While during the few months preceding the former pastor's departure there had been varying levels of disorganization as a result of endings, now the new pastor and key lay leaders will try to establish working relationships around each of the congregation's tasks. Carefully, over their first few months together, pastor and church members will move toward one another learning to accept both the humanness and the divine spark in the lives of each. They will recognize both frailty and strength, vulnerability and power.

A new enchantment will enter this relationship offering the promise that once again individuals and communities of faithful people will be used to fulfill God's purposes within the congregation.

A New Identification

As endings are marked by various types and patterns of dis-identification, new beginnings are characterized by attempts on the part of both pastor and members of the congregation to find ways of identifying with one another. This takes place at two levels. First the pastor and the congregation must gain perspective on the other's general quality and gifts. Only then can it take place at the second level, that of commitments and goals.

A congregation of faithful people develops, over time, a corporate identity which is reflected and maintained through its activities, its way of relating inside and outside the church, and its choices of goals and priorities. A corporate congregational identity can be the result of intentional actions designed to focus energy and spirit or it can be the response to conditions which demand a certain shape to the program and service of that particular group of God's people.

Pastors too develop an identity. This is shaped by mentors and models of ministry that have had a strong influence upon them. It is also formed by experiences with congregations, the impact of theological education, and their own unique personal qualities and characteristics.

In shaping a new pastor/parish relationship both congregation and pastor will expend a lot of energy checking out each other's identity and discovering the potential for the mysterious quality known as "fit."

Congregational Identity: A Sub-Culture

Each congregation has the characteristic of a sub-culture within the larger community of which it is a part. Pastors who have moved from one church to another in the same large city know that. They have come to realize that a church may be a part of the same city, but not necessarily like other churches there. Each has its own set of patriarchs and matriarchs, its own norms and values, its own rights of acceptance and belonging. Each has its favorite stories— legends if you like—which describe the formation, development, identity and essential purpose of the people who are the central core of the congregation. As a sub-culture, the church has worked out its accommodation with the community around it. It has either chosen to reflect or reject the fundamental elements of that community or has found a place somewhere between those two poles. Sometimes the congregation makes those choices over such a long period of time, and with such gradual change that its members are unaware of the particular nature of the relationship. At other times it is only the gradual change in the character and quality of the members in either church or community that makes the definition of sub-culture difficult.

Twenty-five years ago the congregation of Calvary Church sold its building and moved eighteen blocks to a fine "strategic" location much closer to where its people lived, shopped and carried on business. The children of the congregation all went to one of the two schools in the neighborhood and the activities of the congregation's program were definitely for families. The population profile of the church was, to a very high degree, a match with the community. The community leaders were also church leaders, and the people who made decisions for the community were also on the major boards and committees of the congregation. Three of the teachers in the church school were also teachers in the classroom of local schools.

That has all changed.

Now the community profile shows that thirty-five to forty percent of the population is of Asian or East Indian origin, yet not a single Chinese, Pakistani or Korean family participates in the life of the church. The children in the church school—and there are few—represent seven different schools and none of their teachers is a member of the church. Congregational leaders are not civic leaders and more than forty percent of the church's membership lives outside the neighborhoods adjacent to the church building.

It will take some time for a pastor, especially one who arrives at the community during the holiday month of July, to discover the diverse nature and unique patterns of the sub-culture represented by Calvary. This is especially true because many of the self understandings and commonly held images of the members of the congregation assume a relationship with the community, its population and structure, which clearly ended years ago.

Often a pastor's first significant questions are painful challenges to a mythology about the way the church and community relate to one another. One of the finest gifts a congregation could give a new pastor is an accurate, well-documented, evaluated and considered picture of the particular accommodation the congregation has made with its community. A wise pastor asks for such a description *before* becoming committed to a congregation.

Congregational Personality

A congregation has its own personality which reflects a particular identity. That personality has been developed over the years and has evolved as a result of moments together which became benchmarks of meaning. There were also decisions made after a long struggle, and those decisions have taken the form of statements of intent or purpose, or declarations of belief, determination or hope. They are manifestos: statements of confident assurance by a congregation which declares that it knows who it is and what it holds to be true.

Identity is also formed over years of experience relating to the conditions of community and mission. Identity emerges as a congregation responds to regional and global issues and to those elements of culture that raise essential questions of value, integrity and meaning. A church whose core members were adults during the Great Depression has a different understanding of life, organization, relationships and security than does one whose core members were born after 1940. How congregations responded to the optimistic fifties, the troubled sixties, and the inflationary seventies marked them with certain identifying traits. They can change their attitudes and preconceived assumptions, but not easily.

A new pastor steps into a congregation which has a well-defined personality and often an intense sense of identity. Because of the rapid change of the ways in which identity is established and because of the mixture in most congregations of people whose Christian identity has been formed—at least in part—elsewhere, the pastor may encounter a congregational "identity crisis." It may be some months before even the most astute pastor can figure out what part of the congregation's identity is likely to be most influential in its future.

Formative History

History forms identity. The shared experiences of a congregation's life and meaning serve to cluster those elements which collectively form an identity. It is for this reason that many pastors and insightful lay leaders, when beginning a new pastoral relationship, encourage the congregation to undertake a process by which the stories, legends, feelings and attitudes of the past are told, acknowledged and re-examined. Such a process allows both congregational members and the new pastor to discover important facts: what is foundational, what is likely to be sacred, what has been formative, and what may be open for renegotiation.

Traditions Large and Small

In being introduced to his new congregation, a young pastor was puzzled to hear, on numerous occasions over a period of four to five weeks, the same idea expressed in only slightly different terms. "This Presbyterian church isn't quite like any other Presbyterian church."

"What," he wondered, "was he being told?" As time and experience would reveal, he was being told that the "little" tradition—the way of thinking, behaving, expressing beliefs and fundamental attitudes as a congregation—was different in considerable measure from the stereotypical images of the "great" Presbyterian tradition—the denominational tradition of which that congregation was part.[1]

The step from one church which stands in a great theological and denominational tradition to another of the same great tradition does not necessarily assure a pastor of landing on familiar or codified ground.

Discovering Ethos

"There is something about this church that I can't quite identify. It's just a feeling that seems to be warm and caring. It isn't just in what people say or do. It's not only the program or the worship, but it seems to permeate the place."

The words of an elderly church member talking to her new pastor were attempts to define ethos. Ethos is a combination of action and rules, of traditions and the way they are enacted. Ethos is more likely the living spirit of a community than any other definable part

---

[1]For a fuller discussion of the relationship between the large and small traditions in a congregation see *Handbook for Congregational Studies* by Jackson Carroll, Carl Dudley and William McKinney (Nashville: Abingdon, 1986).

of its reality. It is probably not possible to understand ethos and its creation; it may be that to define it would be to destroy it. It is recognized, however, that our response to ethos may be more basic to our acceptance or rejection of a community of people than any other single factor.

A new pastor will not define ethos or appreciably alter its prescribed course in a congregation—not immediately at least. But he or she will feel it, respond to it and have to recognize it as a major force in the process of being accepted into the congregation.

Easy or not, the steps that begin a new ministry will be taken. What matters is that they are taken carefully and in the knowledge that the church is, or ought to be, a community of grace and forgiveness, of acceptance and love. The fact that a congregation has a corporate identity and a collective personality suggests, however, that some considerable time and energy should be given to these matters which will be major factors in the new relationship. Enough is known about the process of beginnings in the relationship between pastor and congregation to ensure that those who care for the church and their part in it can prepare well and move forward wisely.

Pastoral Identity

Scholars and researchers are fascinated by the study of the roles and functions of clergy. Examinations of their findings are useful, but what matters here is the recognition that individual pastors have their own unique perspective on purpose and character of ministry which will profoundly influence the way they work. As members of congregations move toward the beginning of a relationship with a new pastor, they may find it useful to examine at least three aspects of the formation of pastoral identity.

Mentors and Models

"I learned a lot about my pastor when I asked him to tell me about the ministers, teachers and authors who have shaped his thinking about ministry." A wise and deliberate lay leader was offering a clue to the mystery of identity. The conversation that had followed provided insight into one of the most significant aspects of a pastor's self understanding. It would be unwise to assume that a pastor will live out his or her ministry in the shadow of some other person's style, but it would be equally unwise to miss the significant perception which can be gained when we recognize the formative effect of influential role models.

Faith Experience

It is often assumed that pastors have a faith that is pure and whole. Congregational members can be disturbed to discover that there are doubts, uncertainties and problems that lurk on the edges of their pastor's belief system. It is usually far more helpful for purposes of building a sound pastor/parish relationship to accept the fact that there are gaps in the fabric of faith formation in both clergy and laity. In fact an honest appraisal of these can forge a relationship which is based on mutual support and trust and avoid the devastating effects of disappointment and disillusionment.

Some members of congregations have found it stimulating and challenging to learn that their pastor is deliberately striving to strengthen or enrich a part of his or her spiritual quest. This knowledge has also proven fruitful since there are usually men and women in congregations with resources they would gladly share with their pastor if he or she is willing to accept them. Pastors report having received strength, spiritual direction, encouragement and hope through relationships with members of congregations, but this requires mutual trust and a wide view of ministry.

One pastor told of being confused at first but subsequently elated when in an early meeting with lay leaders of her congregation she was asked, "What can we do to help you on your faith journey?" After the initial feeling of "role reversal" the pastor came to realize that she was in the company of people who were going to take their ministry to her seriously and expected the same kind of commitment from her.

Leadership Priorities

Part of the pastoral identity of any clergyperson in the sense that he or she has responsibility to provide various types of leadership. Unfortunately, there is often a lack of clear, precise language with which to discuss this important matter when pastor and congregation first meet.

There are at least eight characteristics of leadership which could be discussed as pastor and lay leaders explore their new relationship and begin to work together. It is difficult to discuss these theoretically, however, and we recommend that they become an ongoing agenda for the committees who are responsible for monitoring the relationship between pastor and congregation.

A congregation needs *inspiration* and *vision*. There will always be those within a congregation whose faith is frail and whose commitment is shallow. Pastors and their congregational leaders will benefit from discussing the ways in which these two important functions of leadership can be provided.

There are continuous needs for *engagement* and *interpretation* for those within a congregation who are beginning to feel increased levels of commitment and involvement. Activities which bring people together around their common search and help them to identify what they are feeling and needing are essential to the growth and nurturing of a congregation.

There are people in every congregation who have a clear grasp of the church's ministry activity and mission focus, so what they need from their pastor is the ministry of *teaching* and *enabling*. A person who has had years of theological training can provide theological and biblical background for the congregation's initiatives in ministry and mission, and should share knowledge of the great tradition of which the congregation is a part. The pastor, working full time at the task of the church's ministry, can develop the program plans, create the necessary structures and provide the appropriate links that enable the ministry of the laity. He or she can influence the flow of ideas and activities thus increasing the effectiveness of lay leaders.

Some people within a congregation are themselves providing strong, conscientious and dedicated leaders in various segments of the church's ministry but they too need the service of a pastoral leader. Pastors can provide *monitoring* and *support* to those who need to be assured that their deep engagement with the purpose and program of the church is appropriately directed and suitably appreciated. Part of the leadership task of the pastor is to see that the various "parts of the body" are coordinated, hence the need for monitoring. Another task is to maintain pastoral concern for those lay leaders who could otherwise come to feel isolated or marginalized because of their consuming commitment. At times those who are most deeply committed in the life of a congregation need the ministry of inspiration and new vision.

As a new ministry begins, members of the congregation do well to invite significant discussion with the pastor about the work of leadership. No one does all eight of the leadership tasks equally well. Each pastor will have some priorities which give him or her a unique quality. A careful deliberation on the strengths and weaknesses of the pastor's gifts and the necessary accommodations to be made by others in the congregation would serve to build a new ministerial relationship on sure foundations.

CHAPTER 7

Re-establishing Pastoral Relationships

Chapter VI has addressed the need for members of congregations and their new pastors to undertake the considerable work involved in discovering and forging a new mutual identification. There is however even more to the reestablishment of the relationship that has been broken with the departure of the former pastor. The new relationship will be nurtured by careful attention to the *engagement* period. It will be deepened and shaped by a process of *reorganization,* and finally, it is hoped, there will come a new *enchantment.*

Engagement

"I began to feel welcome here, even before my family and I arrived." The pastor was reflecting on the feelings engendered by a series of experiences, each of which had delivered an important message and has contributed to the process of engagement.

As a part of endings, pastors, their families and the members of their congregations go through a period of disengagement. As a part of new beginnings they undertake a series of activities that are intended to set a foundation for a long relationship. When the relationship is between a pastor and a congregation, the process of engaging one another happens at a number of levels. To be sure, the congregation *engages* the pastor in the sense of obtaining a contract for services or employment. But they are equally concerned to obtain and hold the *attention* of the pastor just as the pastor becomes concerned to do the same with the congregation.

One of the most common uses of the word engagement suggests the kind of relationship that exists between couples intending to marry; there is some parallel between betrothal and the coming together of pastor and congregation. One of the meanings of the verb "to engage" is to entangle, to involve, to interlock, and all of these words carry special meaning when considered in the context of a pastor/parish relationship. It is possible to see, in each of the following acts of engagement, a special embellishment which is to the engagement phase of a new ministry what a grace note is to a sheet of music. Grace notes in the engagement between pastor and congregation are those things that are not really necessary to the running of the church or the establishing of a relationship, but they are joyous additions to the routine. They are flourishes, and they have the effect of making the task enjoyable when otherwise it might seem overburdening or overwhelming.

For this pastor there had been several such grace notes:

There had been the very thoughtful letter from the chairperson of the Board of Elders, outlining in a humorous but complete way, the detailed plans for moving arrangements.

There were the notes and cards from members of the congregation expressing their pleasure at the news of the appointment and assuring the new pastor and her family that when they arrived there would be a warm welcome.

Then there was the small but symbolically generous check to ease some of the burden of the "extra costs which everybody knows are a part of the expense of moving."

There had been an invitation to dinner with four or five of the member families of the congregation, along with some other new-comers. The invitation had been issued three weeks before the pastor was due to arrive and included the carefully worded addition that the children were welcome. There would be seven or eight other children around the same age at the dinner party too. The "grace note" in that invitation was the care with which the hostess had outlined that the pastor's children would *not* be the only new ones present.

There had been the example of forethought and caring in the letter from the chairman of the worship committee. He had said that since the pastor would be arriving late in the week, arrangements had been made for a senior associate pastor from a neighboring church to "take the service" on the first Sunday. Besides, the note suggested wisely, "It will give you a chance to *meet* us at worship once before you have to *lead* us." That one grace note may have prevented some unnecessary false steps since it would provide time and opportunity for conversations about the way worship was conducted without undue reference to the former pastor.

There was a phone call from a very cheerful chairperson of the "reception committee" who wanted to let the new pastor know that instead of a big "once and for all" reception, a few smaller ones were being planned. She said that at each there would be (a) some stories told about the "formative experiences" in the church's past, (b) a time for each person to have some fun introducing their own families and then present a picture of the family to the new pastor,

(c) a chance for the pastor's family members to say one or two things about themselves—"things we wouldn't find out unless you told us," and (d) lots of singing and ice cream.

The grace notes are obvious: care not to overwhelm, an introduction to the church and its significant history, a relaxed way to be introduced, some time to think about the words to use in self introductions, and the assurance that there would be some help in the important efforts at remembering names and faces. In short, there was planned informality.

Beneath all of this there was a subtle but effective message. It was as if the whole church was saying "We are planning to make you welcome."

Engagement is a two-way matter. For their parts, the new pastor, and his or her spouse and family, can do much to express their feelings about the call or appointment and to prepare the ground for a comfortable beginning.

A growing number of pastors are writing "pastoral letters" in advance of their arrival. These may be brief and in some ways general. If they reflect enthusiasm, an invitation to dialogue and a warmth of spirit, they will probably set a tone for the first face-to-face exchanges. Also such letters can inform the members about some of the pastor's background and experience, as well as some hopes for the future. Such information facilitates an easy first conversation with many in the congregation and encourages an ease of access between the parties.

The letter can set the pastor's life in a context with the rest of his or her family, and introduce something of the way people may expect to find them.

The grace notes and the intentional effort to open communication as quickly as possible serve both the pastor and the members of the congregation well.

Reorganization

With the arrival of a new pastor, a congregation goes through a process of reorganizing. It may not be a conscious process. Many people assume that very little changes in the formal structure and program activity of a congregation but actually there are subtle and even crucial revisions that are accelerated at the time of a pastoral transition. The deliberations that precede the calling of the new pastor are often marked by surprising shifts in the levels of commitment on the part of some leading members, and the congregational behavior pattern may be quite different from the one that existed in the last few months of the former pastoral relationship.

The phenomenon of "oscillation" has been noted in Section I, and its effect on individuals leads them to reorder their commitment to leadership within the church. Some of the groups and individuals who have power within the congregation are realigned accordingly.

Two other interrelated fields of attitude and action provide an important perspective on the kinds of issues that will need to be clarified. If a congregation and its new pastor are to forge a vital alliance based on sound accommodation of their convictions and commitments they will evolve an understanding about the expectations of leadership initiative and the way in which that initiative translates into time and energy in the service of eight recognizable sub-systems in the congregation.

Leadership Initiatives Shifts

Roy Oswald has helpfully identified a problem facing many new pastors in congregations with his description of a leadership style discrepancy.[1] Oswald points out that one pastor may contribute a high level of initiative for program and mission development while the congregation with whom that pastor works tends to be passive, accepting and supportive. To use the language of leadership developed earlier, such a "high initiative" pastoral leadership style is marked by visioning, inspiring, engaging and interpreting. Another pastor may express a lower level of initiative, encouraging members of his or her congregation to take the major role in developing program priorities and mission focus. In that case the pastor may be quite effective in the roles of supporting, monitoring, teaching and enabling. It is important to recognize that neither pastoral style can be solely effective. Congregations can grow to appreciate either style and in fact will assume them to be the norm of pastoral leadership.

When congregations go through a pastoral change they usually experience in the new pastor's initiative something different from that of the former one. Some reorganization then begins. It is based either on a perceived leadership *gap*—that is where a pastor is providing less initiative than was expected—or a leadership initiative *overlap*, where the pastor offers more initiative than may be expected or appreciated.

---

[1] Roy M. Oswald, *The Pastor as Newcomer* (Washington, DC: The Alban Institute, 1977), 11–12.

But reorganization takes place at another level and with a number of variables complicating the situation.

Leadership Initiative and the Sub-Systems

A congregation is a living organism and one way to understand it is to reflect on the various "parts of the body" or "sub-systems" within the larger organizational system.[2] Each part has its own community of people, its own set of concerns, informal structures, priorities and expectations. Congregational members tend to belong to at least one of these sub-systems, either consciously or subconsciously, and in fact may feel that while the other groups are important, the sub-system to which they belong is vital for the identity and function of the church. It becomes important then for members of each sub-system to work out their relationship with their new pastor.

It will help in the work of reorganization to reflect on the way in which each sub-system renegotiates with its pastor, and to consider the level and type of initiative they expect or need.

Eight Sub-Systems

Eight major sub-systems can be discerned within a congregation, and the uniqueness of a church is in some ways defined by the relative strength, priority and emphasis given to each of these sub-systems.

1. Worship and Celebration

This cluster includes people willing to work toward creating and ensuring meaningful worship. They have lots of energy for projects that focus on the place of worship and may have a high commitment to the Sunday service of worship. It probably includes people in the choir, those who are committed to all the visual arts—drama, dance, pictorial and fabric arts, to say nothing of those who arrange flowers. There are also people who will give assistance on special Sundays to decorate, prepare and assemble resources.

For most people in this sub-system, their relationship with the church centers around Sunday and the activities of worship. They may have little commitment to committee work and activities in the life of the congregation that do not directly, or at least indirectly, relate to the worship and celebration experience.

---

[2]One exploration of congregational systems is offered by E. Mensell Pattison in *Pastor and Parish-A Systems Approach*. (Philadelphia: Fortress Press, 1977). Two of the sub-system categories used here are drawn from Pattison's work.

2. Education and Nurture

This sub-system includes those committed to teaching, those leading youth and mid-week groups and those willing to serve on education committees. People in this sub-system are particularly interested in the educational value of liturgy and sermons. Some in this group will be identified with education and nurture, not so much for themselves but for their children or those of friends. These people can both be very supportive and put a great deal of pressure on the people who lead and administer the church's young adult, youth and children's program.

A special group within this sub-system are those whose special concern is that of spiritual development, Bible study and faith formation. These people will express this by a desire for an enriched prayer life, and an obvious focus on the scriptures in preaching, teaching or other activities in the congregation.

3. Communal

People who belong to the communal sub-system are likely to be found actively greeting people at the door of the church, seated near the back of the church where they can see who is present and who is absent. They rise quickly following the worship service to be available in the foyer to greet and connect with many in the congregation.

The people of the communal sub-system are often extremely sensitive and aware of absentee members and adherents, and will be among the last to leave the church after meetings. They can be mistaken for those of the first sub-system because the worship service is a focal point for the communal activities. But they will be as "present" at the congregational meetings, picnics and special events as they are on Sunday morning. They may not be too critical of the sermon or of the music or of the liturgical changes, but could be upset if the service lasts too long. Their high commitment is to the time of fellowship and "networking." People in this sub-system will be concerned if hospital visiting isn't being done. They are often an invaluable part of the informal network that informs members of the congregation and the pastoral team about those who need special pastoral care.

4. Reparative

People in this sub-system will be found in one or more support communities with people who need the church's love. They have the ability to call on people known to be dissatisfied, lonely or fearful. The members of the reparative sub-system may be sensitive to high and low experiences in the membership and can often sense pain in others. They draw into their circle the wounded and frail, the sorrowing and those in turmoil. They may from time to time be out of their depth in crisis situations but their nature is strong enough to be significant in providing hope and strength to those who benefit from their ministry. These people expect the minister to be available for counsel and to be quick to respond to crises in the congregation and community. When a pastoral change takes place, people in the reparative sub-system are often anxious to tell the pastor about those people who have dropped away from the church during the tenure of the former pastor. As reparative people, they are concerned to try to reclaim and rekindle the faith of those who are distant from church life.

5. Maintenance and Sustenance

A number of people in each congregation are basically concerned about maintaining and sustaining the church's life. Some are concerned about the congregation's financial stability, others about the building and property of the church. The buildings must be clean and orderly, and the parsonage well cared for as an image of the church in the community. Some people in the M&S sub-system express their concern from a different point of view. They see the growing or diminishing membership of the congregation as an issue of maintenance or sustenance. Many people upset over rapid congregational decline or overly enthused about rapid congregational growth may not be concerned from an evangelical viewpoint. They are anxious about the continuity of the congregation. New members mean to them more assurance of maintenance and stability and loss of members threatens both of these.

Some people who resist change in worship times, patterns of liturgy and mid-week programs are actually most worried that what "was" will be no more and that the strong sense of the need for support, viability and stability of the church may be threatened by change. On the other hand, people in the M&S sub-system may encourage change if they see patterns of decline and diminishing strength in the congregation.

6. Transient and/or Transitional

Some people who belong to the church do not expect to remain too long in that community or in that particular station in life, but are anxious to have an effect on the institutions and communities to which they belong. People in this sub-system will be open to change, indeed, perhaps vocal in recommending it. On the other hand, they may resist change if they think the community to which they have attached themselves is acceptable as it is. Some transient people do not want to deal with change since they are not sure they will be there long enough to see it thorough.

Some people in the transient or transitional sub-system may tend to be less sensitive to those who have a concern for history, tradition and the past, and they may also be somewhat restless if pastor and congregation seem less than flexible and creative in both programing and worship. Those people may be quite creative and spontaneous and add brightness and ingenuity to activities, meetings and programs of the congregation. Frequently, the congregation sends strong messages to the people of this sub-system. The message may be "we don't accept you until you've been around awhile." Other congregations have found a way to say "we can get a great deal from your experience and insight and we don't want to wait for years to hear from you or to take advantage of your knowledge." The way in which a congregation responds to its transient or transitional sub-system says a great deal about how that congregation will respond to change, leadership initiative and, in some cases, a new pastor.

7. Evangelism

For many the church is truly the church when it is involved in reaching beyond itself to respond to the spiritual needs of the unchurched. People in the evangelism sub-system are likely to be concerned about whether or not the sermon, the church's program and other activities of the congregation are directed outward toward those who do not at present express an interest in the faith or the life of the congregation.

People in the evangelism sub-system tend to be those whose personal faith is vibrant and openly expressed, and whose conversation quickly reveals that their faith and Christian experience are a major source of strength in making decisions and building relationships.

People in this sub-system express a deep concern for those who do not enjoy the rich Christian experience they have embraced and they are concerned if the "image" of the church is not one which reflects that overt commitment to evangelistic outreach.

8. Outreach

One sub-system within each congregation consists of those people who believe that the church exists for others and that it is at its best

when it is reaching out to those who have been wounded, who suffer, who are marginalized or otherwise disadvantaged.

People in this sub-system will be concerned if the sermon,
church program, budget and other symbols of the church's mission
and ministry are not directed outward rather than inward. They will
be aware of the social concerns and issues of the day and will want
those issues expressed as the focus for the church's ministry. For
people with an outreach commitment, it will matter less what happens in the worship service and in the church school than what
happens when the congregation is dispersed and serving in the
wider community.

The Pastors and the Sub-Systems

The messages that are received by a new pastor in early conversations with a congregation can be very confusing. It is partly because
the sub-systems are not always decisively defined. People who feel
they are committed to "evangelism" for instance may be reflecting
their anxiety about the maintenance and sustenance of the congregation. Or they may be concerned for the community (the communal sub-system) or for recovering former members and adherents (the reparative sub-system). This confusion is often most acute
when it comes to interest in worship and celebration. While worship is the most obvious time of congregational activity, comments
about it are not necessarily the best indicators of the priorities of
the members.

It is important to recognize that the pastor hears comments
from many members of the congregation in a given week. Without
a sense of the sub-systems to which these people belong, most of
these comments are taken as the attitude of an appreciable number
of members in the congregation. While indeed they may be representative, it is useful to recognize them as representative of "a certain sub-system" and therefore to be understood in that context.
Members of the education and nurture sub-system, for instance may
be quite vocal about the needs, opportunities and concerns that
belong to that sub-system. Their attitudes, however, are not to be
construed as those that should lead to action which eliminates service and ministry in other areas.

The qualified and careful pastor will assess "representative"
examples of things she or he hears, and try to pay attention to
whether or not the message is coming from one or other of the
sub-systems.

When a new pastor comes to a congregation, he or she often
has to deal with the readjustment of sub-system priorities based on

the feelings and attitudes of those who have assessed their relationship with a former pastor. Some, after such an assessment, decide they want more of the new pastor's active and intentional leadership than they had from a former pastor. Others decide they want less of the new pastor's time and activity. In one sense then there is a "leadership initiative ratio" negotiation that must go on with each of the sub-systems. In the early conversations between a pastor and his or her congregation a frank and open discussion about quality and strength, the commitments and focus of each of the sub-systems would be extremely helpful in assisting these negotiations.

Some Other Factors

It is possible that the style of one pastor is not what is wanted or expected in the next one, but that fact is hardly ever universally felt within a congregation. Therefore the new pastor often receives mixed messages about appropriate leadership style.

It is also possible that lay leaders may change their expectations about leadership initiative with the change of a pastor. If they have been more passive in the former relationship they may begin to be assertive with a new pastor. Again, the pastor may be confused by the reports of "what was" when confronted with the observations of "what is."

Pastors and the appropriate committees and groups will find that an open and intentional discussion of these ideas will serve to deepen the relationship between pastor and congregation in the earliest months of their life together.

Enchantment

To describe the relationship between a pastor and a congregation in terms of enchantment may seem at first to be a strange juxtaposition of ideas. Enchantment usually involves something of a mysterious quality, a casting of a spell or charm which bewitches or delights.

Where congregations and pastors have worked out their mutual ministry over a period of years, and where they have come to value the strengths and vitality in one another and shared weaknesses and vulnerability, there is in fact a mystical quality in the bond between them. It is unlike any other affiliation. It cannot be equated with the connection between doctor and patient even though health and healing are a concern of the ministry. It is not a parallel with the lawyer/client association though truth and justice are of serious concern in ministry. It is not to be equated with the teacher/student relationship though ministry does concern itself with knowledge and skill, with nurture and growth. Ministry is not fully understood in terms of the social-worker/client association for while compassion and caring are central to the functioning of ministry there is inherently far more to that mysterious union of pastor and people.

The ways in which a pastor and congregation bond with one another are intricate and variable. They defy definition. The uniqueness in that bonding may well be partially explained by the fact that all parties in the union know that the community of which they are a part is not entirely of their making, nor does it rely solely on them for its survival. They are therefore free to depend upon the church for spiritual, social and emotional support even as they contribute their own strength and service to it.

Images of the church abound yet none fully satisfies or explains the phenomenon which so powerfully engages the lives and emotions, the attitudes and intentions of its leaders. The church is a mystery and the symbiotic relationship which is forged between those who are called to serve it and those who are called to service from within it is also mysterious. When God works God's miracle and the pastor and congregation are brought together to sojourn for a while, there is indeed at least the possibility that both could be "delighted completely," which is the American Heritage Dictionary's definition of enchantment. The chemistry that makes it happen will surely and forever remain a mystery. We do well to analyze what we can, clarify what we know, do our best to proceed wisely and thank God for the climate of grace, hope, forgiveness and trust that makes it possible.

A Parable

A certain actor, with experience and training, was offered a most challenging test by a wise director.

The actor was informed that he was to remain in the dressing room until the middle of the second act of a play he had never read or rehearsed. On a cue from the director, he was to walk on stage and begin to act.

At the appropriate time, the cue was given, and the actor entered stage left. At first the scenery bore a slight resemblance to a set in which he had played a starring role. He immediately assumed that role, but the other actors on stage seemed confused and even irritated. He soon fell silent. He then noticed that some of the actors appeared to be dressed in a costume similar to that used in another play in which he had had a major role. As he assumed that role, one of the actors left in disgust and another looked at him pityingly. After trying two or three other roles, familiar to him from the past, he concluded none of them quite suited the set, the costumes, or the lines being offered by the others on the stage.

He then "stepped out of character" and asked one of the actors if he could be told what was going on. The other actors gathered round and each told him something of what had been the play's action to the point of his entrance. "Well, what were you going to do when I came on stage?" he asked. "That's the strange thing," they said, "we didn't have any more script. The story wasn't ended but we didn't know what was to happen next." "Well, what am I supposed to do?" asked the actor. One of the members of the cast suggested an answer. "Perhaps with your experience and training you could help us find a satisfactory conclusion to the second act."

They then began to work at their new task, and the curtain remained up. They went back over the story as it had unfolded in the first act. They laughed and enjoyed the pleasure of remembering the mistakes they had made and the deeply emotional moments in the scenes that had led up to the arrival of the new actor. They examined the scenery and the staging plan and decided that there were some clues in the context to suggest some future direction. The experienced actor reminded them of some of the major themes of love, reconciliation, justice, peace, compassion, forgiveness, judgment, and grace. The actors then took account of the people on stage and decided how they would continue to perform with some reshaping of their roles.

They suggested lines to each other, and together they began to interact to the delight of everyone.

The curtain fell to end the second act.

When the curtain went up again, all the actors were on stage except the one who had entered in the middle of the second act. The cast seemed puzzled and a little disorganized, and then there appeared from stage left another experienced and well-trained actor. At first she assumed the character of a number of roles she had played elsewhere, but the cast seemed confused and slightly irritated. Eventually, however . . . .